WEALTH BEYOND MONEY

The Balance of Your Health, Relationships & Finance

Immanuel Ezekiel & Julie Hogbin

© Copyright 2023 - All rights reserved.

The content contained within this book may not be reproduced, duplicated or transmitted without direct written permission from the author or the publisher.

Under no circumstances will any blame or legal responsibility be held against the publisher, or author, for any damages, reparation, or monetary loss due to the information contained within this book, either directly or indirectly.

Legal Notice:

This book is copyright protected. It is only for personal use. You cannot amend, distribute, sell, use, quote or paraphrase any part, or the content within this book, without the consent of the author or publisher.

Disclaimer Notice:

Please note the information contained within this document is for educational and entertainment purposes only. All effort has been executed to present accurate, up to date, reliable, complete information. No warranties of any kind are declared or implied. Readers acknowledge that the author is not engaged in the rendering of legal, financial, medical or professional advice. The content within this book has been derived from various sources. Please consult a licensed professional before attempting any techniques outlined in this book.

By reading this document, the reader agrees that under no circumstances is the author responsible for any losses, direct or indirect, that are incurred as a result of the use of the information contained within this document, including, but not limited to, errors, omissions, or inaccuracies.

TABLE OF CONTENTS

Introduction 1

Chapter 1: True Wealth in Abundance 13
Balancing Your Life 18
Current Wheels of Life: 21
The Health Wheel 22
The Relationships Wheel 22
The Financial Wheel 23
The Combined Balance Wheel 23

Chapter 2: Build a Healthy Relationship with Yourself 27
The Benefits of Building a Loving Relationship with Yourself 30
Being in an Unhealthy Relationship with Yourself 32

Chapter 3: The Concept of Blueprint 35
Nature Versus Nurture 36
Types of Blueprints 39
    Basic Life Blueprint 39
    Self-Image Blueprint 40
    Health Blueprint 41
    Relationship Blueprint 43
    Career Blueprint 44
    Money Blueprint 45
Myths of a Blueprint 46
Universal Blueprints 47
Invisible Script 48
Like Father, Like Son—Like Mother, Like Daughter 49

Chapter 4: Understanding How Your Blueprint Is Formed 51
Stages of Life 53
Identity and Ego 60
Values: How Do They Affect Your Results? 63
Questions to Help You Assess Your Blueprint 65
The Exercise 66
Self-Relationship 67
Health 68
Nutrition 69
Relationships 70
Career 71
Business 72
Finance 72
Exercise: Understanding How Your Blueprint Is Formed 74

Chapter 5: Why Change? 77
Change Is Constant 77
What Stops Change? 79
Top 5 Regrets of the Dying 84
Problem—Research—Solution 87
The Change Curve — The Emotional Effect 89
The Benefits of Change 98

Chapter 6: How to Change 101
Reprogramming Your Mind 102
Constant Learning 109
Vision Leads to Focus 110
Set Aspirational Goals 112
Implement Boundaries 113
Set Healthy Boundaries 114
Manage Your Time Effectively 117
Develop a Growth Mindset 118

Chapter 7: The Ideal Way to Balance Your Life 119
Secrets to a Balanced Life 124
Prioritise Self-Care 125
Cultivate Healthy Relationships 126
Pursue Hobbies and Interests 126
Practise Gratitude 127
Deep Breathing and Meditation 128
Exercise 130
Build Positive Associations 132
Manage Your Finances 136

Chapter 8: Leverage and How It Will Help You 139
Types of Leverage 140
    Knowledge Leverage 140
    People Leverage 141
    Time Leverage 141
    Technology and Tools Leverage 142
    Personal Leverage 142
    Mentoring and Coaching Leverage 143
    Finance Leverage 143

Chapter 9: Create Your New Blueprints 145
Determine Your Health Blueprint 145
Determine Your Emotional Health Blueprint 151
Identify Your Relationship Blueprint 152
Self-Relationship 154
Romantic Relationship 158
Knapp Relationship Model 167
Business Relationship Blueprint 171
Your Money Blueprint 174
Define Couple's Money Blueprint 177
Powerful Tips for Financial Success 179
The Cashflow Quadrant 185
Cashflow Quadrant and the 21st Century 193

Chapter 10: Health Is Wealth 197
Benefits of a Healthy Life 198
Boost Your Physical Health 201
Love Your Mental Health 205
Master Your Emotional Health 210
   The 3 Steps to Mastery 211
Enhance Your Social Health 214

Chapter 11: Creating Meaningful Relationships 219
Basis of a Healthy Relationship 220
Maintain a Healthy Relationship with Your Partner 223
Build Business Relationships 228

Chapter 12: Power of Money 231
Characteristics of Money 233
Digitalisation and Crypto 237
Achieve Financial Freedom 241
Benefits of Financial Leverage 246
   The Benefits of Gearing 246

Chapter 13: The Magic of Compounding 253
Compounding Across Health, Relationships, and Finance 254
Compounding Finances 256
Understanding Compound Interest and Inflation 258
The Snowball Effect 259

Chapter 14: Impact of True Wealth 263
You Have Control of Your Life 263
You Set and Achieve Goals 271
Wealth Beyond Money Wellness Is Multi-Dimensional 281
The Impact of Wealth Beyond Money 283
A brief reminder! 285
- Healthy Lifestyle 285
- Healthy Relationships 286
- Strong Finances 286

Now, Remember Chapter 4 286
- Exercise: Create That Plan 286

Conclusion 289

About the Authors 295
Immanuel Ezekiel 295
- Client Testimonials 297

Julie Hogbin 300
- Client Testimonials 304

Why We Created the Book 306

References 309
Image References 317

INTRODUCTION

In *Wealth Beyond Money,* the true meaning of "Wealth" and "Abundance" goes way beyond what most people think. True Wealth is more than just an account balance or physical possessions. It's an overall state of abundance and comprehensive wellness that encompasses every aspect of your life. It is about finding balance in your life—your Health, Relationships, and Finances.

Without this harmonious balance, parts of your life can suffer, like your physical and mental well-being, as well as your personal connections with others and yourself.

Imagine a symphony where every note blends perfectly, creating a beautiful melody. However, when the balance is disrupted, it is like a discordant note that throws everything off. It can leave you feeling drained, emotionally, physically, and mentally, and strain your relationships.

IMMANUEL EZEKIEL & JULIE HOGBIN

Wealth Beyond Money is here to guide you on this transformative journey. Together, we will uncover the secrets of true wealth and forge a path where abundance flows effortlessly, in every aspect of your life. It is not just about material riches; it is also about the tangible and intangible treasures that light up your life and soul.

We will dive deep into the power of balance, where your well-being radiates with vitality, your relationships flourish with love and connection, and your financial goals align with your passions. True wealth isn't about chasing isolated achievements—it's about seeking holistic fulfilment. We will question your norm, challenge your preconceived notions, and in the process, equip you with a robust, all-encompassing understanding, of what it means to be *Wealthy Beyond Money*.

On this transformative journey, we will uncover the proven principles of *Wealth Beyond Money*. Together, we will redefine what it means to be truly wealthy and embark on a quest for abundance that goes beyond whatever currency you are thinking of or using. Whenever referenced in this book in pounds, substitute the currency of your own country, such as dollars, euros, yen, etc. Embrace the magic that unfolds when vibrant health, meaningful relationships, and financial abundance come together.

The importance of taking a holistic approach to increasing your wealth was emphasised by the Dalai Lama XIV.

When he was asked, what surprised him the most about humanity, he famously answered, "Man. Because he sacrifices his health in order to make money, then he sacrifices money to recover his health. And then he is so anxious about the future that he does not enjoy the present; the result being that he does not live in the present or the future; he lives as if he is never going to die, and then dies having never really lived".

Take a moment to reflect on your life and how you are currently living it. Are you solely focused on accumulating money in your bank account and not truly experiencing life to its fullest? It is important to realise that being too fixated on money can have a negative impact on your health and your relationships. You may find yourself isolating from others, which can take a toll on your physical, emotional, and mental well-being.

> **Remember:** having money without strong relationships and good health can leave you feeling poor, regardless of the amount in your bank account.

On the other hand, you might be prioritising your relationships above your financial means. You may be indulging in activities or events that are beyond your budget just to please others. While your relationships may flourish in the short term, neglecting your most important relationship—with yourself—can lead to unnecessary stress and financial worries. Over time, this stress can take a deep toll on your physical, emotional, and mental health.

> *Remember*: Having great relationships without good health or financial stability can leave you feeling poor.

Alternatively, you might be living a health-conscious lifestyle where you carefully consider the impact of every decision on your well-being. This includes socialising with friends and spending money. While being mindful of your health is important, excessively worrying about the consequences of your choices—physically, mentally, and emotionally—may lead you to decline invitations, or even pass up on career opportunities and may lead to mental health concerns.

While you may enjoy a stress-free life and improved health, the absence of money and relationships can still leave you feeling poor. It is important to note that while being health-conscious is commendable, finding a balance that allows for meaningful social engagement, personal growth, and exploration is equally vital. Flexibility, open-mindedness, and adapting health practices to suit different situations can help you strike a harmonious balance between personal well-being and seizing valuable opportunities in work, travel or society.

> *Remember*: There is not one shape, one size, one age, one amount of money, or one relationship that creates the *perfect* picture of True Wealth. True Wealth is as unique to you as you are in the world, and there are some commonalities that we want to uncover for you.

It is crucial to find a balance in these areas. True wealth goes beyond money alone. It involves nurturing your relationships, taking care of your health, and managing your finances responsibly. When all these elements align harmoniously, you can truly experience a rich and fulfilling life.

> *Remember*: Wealth is not just about numbers in a bank account; it's about the quality of your experiences, the love you give and receive, and the well-being you cultivate within yourself.

Our goal is not to tell you what to think or how to act but to inspire you to think differently, to question, and to explore. The intent is to help you discover your own version of wealth, because, at the end of the day, wealth is not about the number of zeros in your bank account but the richness in your relationships, the vibrancy of your health, the strength of your mind, and the happiness that these dimensions can bring into your life.

We each have a different starting point, and what success looks like for one of you is not the same as for the next person. This is as good a place as any to mention "comparison." Only ever compare positively, as in, "How did that person manage to achieve that?" Rather than "they land promotions, and they are favourites, and I'm here, stuck on the same rung of the ladder, going nowhere." Rather than staying stuck, flip and reframe that thought and action and learn how to do the thing you desire.

Each of you is a unique individual on your own extraordinary journey through life. Regardless of where you currently stand on your path, whether you are young or old, no matter your gender, race, colour, or religion, the principles and insights shared in this book will empower you to enhance and accelerate your journey towards *Wealth Beyond Money*. Be ready to unlock your true potential and create a life of abundance and fulfilment.

To do this, we will start by discussing what true wealth truly is and why it is important that you make the necessary changes to achieve it. Then we will explain why you should create a personalised blueprint for how you want to live your life with the goal of gaining true *Wealth Beyond Money* and how you can go about creating your own upgraded blueprint.

Also, how the power that money holds on you and why it is so important for you to take control, as well as the magical impact and difference in your life of the compounding effect, how you go about improving your health and relationships, and the impact that *Wealth Beyond Money* will have on all the various aspects of your life.

In *Wealth Beyond Money*, we'll discuss proven principles and habits that will help you create the correct balance in your life. The principles and habits explained in this book have been designed after more than 60 years of combined experiences studying human behaviour, communication, wealth creation, improving health, and developing relationships.

Remember: Creating *Wealth Beyond Money* is built on the bedrock of confidence, curiosity, knowledge, and change.

Confidence, because without belief in your abilities, you are like a ship adrift in an ocean, tossed about by the waves of uncertainty. Confidence is not about possessing all the answers but about having the courage to seek them. It is about making mistakes, learning from them, and growing stronger.

Curiosity, the driving force that propels you forward, sparks the desire to uncover what is around the next bend, urging you to delve deeper into the treasures that lie within you and the world around you.

Knowledge, as it forms the compass that will guide you towards your desired destination.

The path to true wealth doesn't need a grim face or a stern attitude. It can be filled with laughter, good-nature, and fun. This book isn't about becoming a health guru, a relationship whisperer, or a financial wizard overnight.

It is about adding joy and a sprinkle of humour to your pursuit of comprehensive wealth. It is about embracing the slips, the falls, and the triumphant moments of getting back up with a smile.

> **Alert**: There may be just a few bad habits you need to throw away, and that is where change plays a big part.

We encourage you to approach this exploration with an open and curious mind, an open heart, and the readiness to change what you may need to change.

This book is neither a quick fix nor a shortcut to immense riches but a roadmap to help you navigate the dynamic landscape of true wealth.

We have both walked a long path to arrive at the wisdom that we will be sharing with you on these pages. We can assure you that we were not born with an innate understanding of these truths, but through life, through learning, through mistakes and successes, along with an enduring curiosity and relentless quest for knowledge and to become *better*, we have come to understand the multi-faceted nature of true wealth, creating Wealth Beyond Money.

Helping you achieve true wealth matters deeply to us. We have first-hand experience of not being in balance with our own health, relationships, and finances, and we have worked with people from all walks of life to help them improve their lives and create their own true wealth in these areas. We know this is possible for anyone willing to adopt the proven principles and take the necessary action, and *Wealth Beyond Money* will act as your guide. We also know it is an ongoing fluid process that requires ongoing attention, and living in the real world, that attention can slip on occasions.

> ***Remember:*** Even before you consume this book, you may very well want to revisit it again and again. Please read through it once, and we assure you, that some *bits* will resonate with you more than others.

Some *bits* will speak to you, and others not so much — each one of you will take your own lessons, and the lessons you learn will relate to where you are currently, and of course, where you are today, may not be where you will be next month.

Life is a marathon, not a race. Technology has given us the illusion that we can get everything we want quickly. True wealth and balance are achieved over time with great habits that are created and built upon.

We also both live in the real world and recognise and acknowledge that change is constant and that you and we cannot control everything and everybody; therefore, we look at what we can control and what we can influence within our own lives and environments. It helps maintain our focus and your focus on proactive and empowering transformation.

If you read a passage and you think, *I am sure I read something similar earlier,* take note, for it will be the message delivered in an alternate context, and it is so good, we wrote it twice.

"Life truly begins to align in our favour, when we acknowledge that our choices, not circumstances, define our path, when we embrace personal responsibility and power and take ownership of our journey.

It is in the act of accepting control over our values, beliefs, thoughts, and behaviours that we unlock the power to create our destiny."

CHAPTER 1:
True Wealth in Abundance

---

*The greatest wealth is health, the greatest treasure is contentment,
and the greatest medicine is a true friend.*

–Buddha

When you think about wealth, you might automatically think of a bank account filled with money. While financial stability is a crucial component of life, it is just the tip of the iceberg. Anything that brings joy into your life—whether it's resources, valuable possessions, health, emotional well-being, or meaningful relationships—makes up the harmonious balance that all contributes to your overall wealth. It is all about thriving in all aspects of life and finding the perfect balance.

Breaking this down further and looking at valuable possessions. Is it just money, or could it be something even more precious? While some of these may show your wealth on a financial level, such as having your own house or car, other possessions may fulfil your emotional needs, such as a photo album filled with happy memories and healthy times spent with people you care about. This physical album doesn't hold any financial value; however, the emotional value it brings to your life will contribute to your overall wealth. The beauty of wealth is that it takes on many forms, and it is up to you to define what it means to you. Unleash your full potential and create wealth that encompasses all the aspects of your life that will bring you happiness and fulfilment.

Health is the cornerstone of true wealth. It encompasses your physical, mental, and emotional well-being, and should always be a top priority. Do not make the mistake of sacrificing your health for money; it will most likely shorten your life and the quality of your life in the long run. Instead, put your health first and engage in good daily habits that keep you feeling at your best. Nourish your body with fresh, nutritious foods, stay active with regular exercise, find joy in activities that bring balance to your life, and ensure you give your body enough time to rest. By prioritising your health, you will not only enhance your overall well-being, but you will also lay the foundation for long-lasting wealth in all areas of your life.

Steve Jobs, the co-founder of Apple, once said, "I have looked in the mirror every morning and asked myself: "'If today were the last day of my life, would I want to do what I am about to do today?' And whenever the answer has been 'no' for too many days in a row, I know I need to change something" (Stanford News, 2005).

Steve Jobs also stated that he would trade all of his money for just one more day of good health and that he regretted not spending more time with his family.

One of the most successful people of his generation, Steve Jobs, would give up all of his money in favour of improved health and relationships. This again proves why, even with millions of pounds or dollars in your bank account, your health is much more valuable than your money. The valuable lesson is, that you are poor if you don't have good health or people to support and love you.

Relationships play a crucial role in our lives and will have a major impact on our wealth. This is why it is so important to surround yourself with positive and supportive people who will encourage and motivate you on your journey towards wealth. Whether it's family, friends, mentors, or like-minded individuals, having a strong support system is essential for achieving success. These relationships will provide you with the inspiration, motivation, and guidance you need to reach your goals and build a life of abundance. Do not be afraid to invest in your relationships and seek out those who will support and uplift you in your journey towards true wealth.

Your spirit encompasses your personal growth, relationships, emotional intelligence, love, and connection with the world around you. These aspects of your life have a powerful impact on your well-being. This is why it is so crucial to be intentional about the people and experiences that fill your life. Emotional intelligence and strong relationships are vital components of wealth, as they bring a sense of fulfilment and happiness that money simply cannot buy. By nurturing your spirit and investing in these important areas of your life, you will create wealth that extends far beyond your finances. It's all about embracing the richness of life and cultivating a spirit that is thriving, connected, and full of love.

The final philosophy of wealth is about financial acumen, growth, and maintenance, where money takes centre stage. This is arguably the most obvious element of wealth. This is where you have the opportunity to grow your wealth in a tangible and meaningful way. With a sound financial strategy in place, you will build wealth that lasts, and that will create a secure foundation for a life full of choices and possibilities.

However, it is crucial to keep in mind that financial prosperity is only one part of the wealth puzzle. To attain true wealth, you should work in harmony with the other two philosophies to find a good balance between all three of them. Building true wealth requires a blend of practical knowledge, creativity, and imagination. It is about designing a life that aligns with your values and helps you achieve your goals.

To do this, you need to set financial objectives, establish a budget, invest in your future, and plan for the long term. You should never let your finances control you. Instead, take charge and embrace a wealth mindset that empowers you to design the life you truly want. With focus, determination, and the right strategies in place, you will create the wealth and fulfilment you deserve. Unleash your potential and start building the life of your dreams today!

Increasing your financial and emotional IQ is a key ingredient to building wealth and achieving success. Continuously learning and developing yourself will help you reach your goals and expand your horizons. Investing in yourself, both in terms of personal power and acquiring new skills, is an important step in building wealth. Seek out professional help, mentorship, and guidance from those who have already achieved success in areas that interest you. Embrace the power of lifelong learning and unlock your full potential. Whether it's through taking courses, attending workshops, or seeking out the advice of experts, investing in your education is an investment in your future. Start your journey to *Wealth Beyond Money* today and never stop growing.

Balancing Your Life

True wealth is not measured in money or possessions, but in the relationships, we build and the positive impact we have on others.

Creating *Wealth Beyond Money* is about finding the perfect balance between your health, relationships, and financial prosperity. It is about allowing yourself to shine, and creating magic for yourself and those you love and cherish. When you create balance—and you can, as many do—you are able to enjoy every moment and experience success in all aspects of your life.

It's perfectly normal to be out of balance, feel like you are being pulled in different directions, and feel overwhelmed. It is undeniable that life will throw curveballs in your direction and that your focus will be pushed into an unbalanced mode. When you are out of balance in any area, it will impact your life and affect the quality of your life. For example, neglecting your physical and mental health will lead to health problems, lower energy levels, and decreased overall well-being. As long as your imbalance does not continue for long, it can easily be corrected and brought back into balance. This is the case in all three aspects of your life. However, balance is completely within your reach once you start to give it the correct focus and attention.

To achieve this balance, it's important to invest in each area of your life with time, energy, and effort. Create harmony and balance as part of the journey as you thrive in life. Invest in yourself, and watch as the balance, in health, great relationships, money, and happiness come into your life.

Financial instability and debt are two of the highest causes of stress and anxiety, and they put strain on your personal or business relationships. Financial hardship is one of the major factors in relationship breakdowns and may also detrimentally impact your mental and emotional well-being. This financial instability may well lead to or trigger feelings of loneliness and isolation.

Think about a set of old-fashioned scales, with each weight representing different parts of your life. Keeping the scales balanced means making sure that all parts of your life are receiving the attention they need. This means you need to keep checking your life to maintain the balance needed to create wealth. Adjusting the scales to make sure you spend enough time and energy on every aspect of your life.

This takes practice; however, it will absolutely be worth your time and effort. Balancing your life is an ongoing journey. Control and influence what you can and learn to let go of everything you cannot control. Control yourself, for in reality that is the only thing you can control and is your solid power base. Your power extension is your influence over others and your circumstances. If you waste time in areas you cannot control or influence, you will create an imbalance in your life and waste your energy.

Current Wheels of Life:

In the pursuit of true *Wealth Beyond Money*, it is vital to maintain a harmonious balance across various aspects of your life. Picture in your mind four wheels, each representing a key area: health, relationships, finance, and the combined balance of health, relationships, and finance.

Imagine visualising different areas of your life as wheels, each with a scale from 0 at the centre to 10 at the outer edge. A score of 0 indicates you haven't even begun or that your current situation is extremely poor and unbalanced. On the other hand, a score of 10 means you have achieved perfect balance and are completely content with where you are.

Now, take a moment to honestly assess where you are currently in each of these areas. Let's explore the significance of each wheel and how it relates to your life journey:

The Health Wheel

This wheel embodies your physical, emotional, and mental well-being. Take a sincere assessment of your health, fitness, and overall vitality. Are you prioritising the care of your body and mind? Assign yourself a score between 0 and 10, reflecting the level of abundance you experience in your health.

The Relationships Wheel

This wheel symbolises the quality of your connections with loved ones, friends, and colleagues. Consider the depth of trust, support, and fulfilment in your relationships. Are you actively nurturing meaningful connections? Give yourself a score from 0 to 10, representing the level of abundance in your relationships.

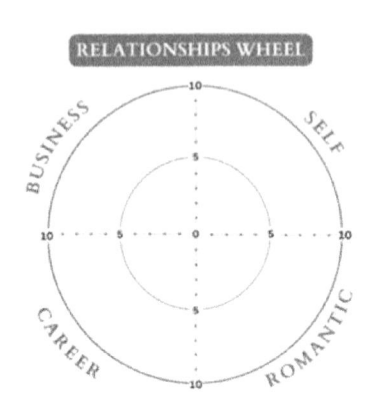

The Financial Wheel

This wheel signifies your financial success and abundance. Evaluate your financial situation, including income, savings, and investments. Are you effectively managing your finances and pursuing opportunities for growth? Score yourself from 0 to 10, honestly assessing your level of abundance in wealth.

The Combined Balance Wheel

This wheel represents the average score derived from the health, relationships, and wealth wheels. It depicts the overall balance and harmony in your life. Reflect on how aligned these areas are and how they complement one another. Give yourself a score that reflects the level of abundance and balance you currently experience.

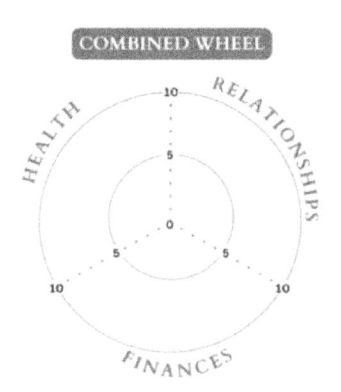

Now, imagine placing these four wheels onto your personal "car" of life. Take a moment to visualise the image. Are all the wheels uneven, causing an uncomfortable and bumpy ride? This represents your unbalanced life. Conversely, if the four wheels are equal and balanced, even if they need a bit more air, your journey will be smooth and steady, showcasing the harmonious integration of your health, relationships, and finances.

Keep in mind that higher scores on the wheels indicate greater abundance in each respective area of your life. When all areas of your score are high, you will cover more ground and experience heightened happiness, health, and financial abundance throughout your journey.

To help you envision this concept more clearly, look at the image below, depicting the four wheels representing health, relationships, finance, and balance:

This visual representation is to help you truthfully assess your current state and inspire you to work towards achieving the balance and abundant life you desire.

Remember: true wealth extends far beyond monetary measures and encompasses holistic well-being and fulfilment.

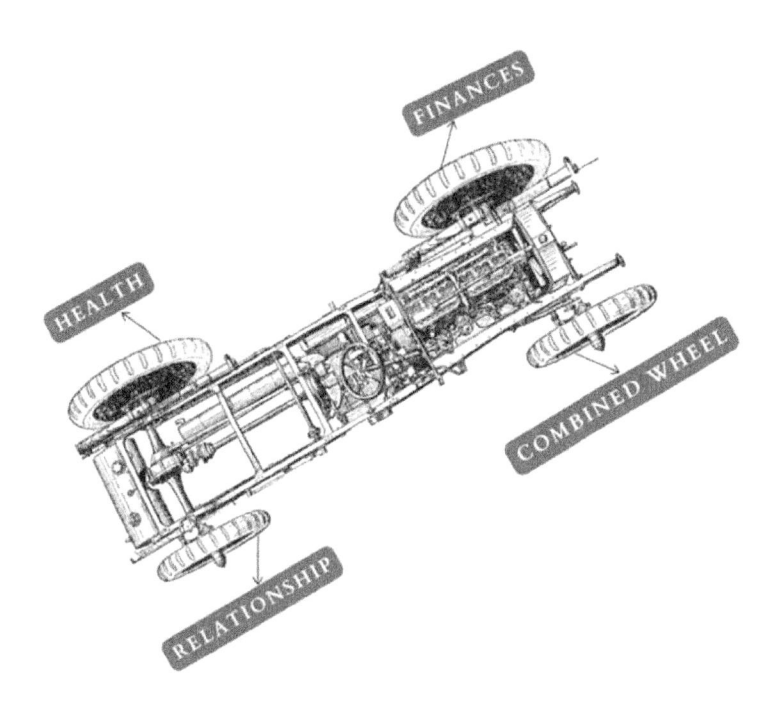

Now, take a moment to evaluate your wheel scores and reflect on any areas that require attention and improvement. Let the vision of a balanced and abundant life ignite a fire within you to take action and create positive changes. Embrace the journey towards true wealth in all aspects of your life, knowing that your efforts will lead to greater joy, health, and prosperity.

CHAPTER 2:
Build a Healthy Relationship with Yourself

Your relationship with yourself is the most important one you will ever have because it is the foundation for everything else in your life.

By knowing yourself, you understand your needs, desires, values, and beliefs, which help you make better decisions for yourself, your health, your external relationships, and your finances. This allows you to form meaningful connections with others, and one thing is for sure: None of you get through this life on your own—even if you are not currently in a personal relationship.

It is like taking care of a plant—if you nourish it, it grows strong and healthy. The same goes for you. When you take care of your physical, emotional, and mental health, you become resilient and better able to handle life's challenges.

You also build self-confidence, which gives you the strength to stand up for what you believe in any situation.

When you are comfortable with yourself, you set clear and healthy boundaries in all your relationships.

Your real and true personal happiness and satisfaction come from within, and self-care is not selfish; understanding yourself is a key part of that. You can gain a form of happiness from material objects; of course, you can. Who doesn't like a new car with that smell or a vacation to see something that inspires them? They are fleeting moments in a long life—without true personal happiness, there is always the possibility of chasing the next shiny thing, living in a self-created world of immediate gratification, and keeping up with the "joneses."

Remember: Your relationship with yourself plays a major role in shaping everything in your life.

To build a healthy relationship with yourself, it's essential to learn to prioritise your own needs. This means not allowing others to mistreat you, ignore your needs, or take advantage of you. It involves understanding that your needs matter and may outweigh the needs of others, including your partner, child, parent, or best friend. Once you have your relationship with yourself secure, you will say yes and no for the right reasons, and you will intentionally use the words—because you know.

Learning to love yourself, and for some, starting with liking yourself, may well be a journey in itself. However, it is one you must take if you truly want to have *Wealth Beyond Money*. We cannot express strongly enough how important this is to achieve, and it does not matter what age you are when you start and start you must.

The Benefits of Building a Loving Relationship with Yourself

1. **Self-awareness and understanding**: Understanding yourself, your needs, and your desires is the foundation of all personal growth. This self-understanding allows you to establish better connections with others and to make decisions that truly align with your values and aspirations.

2. **Self-care and well-being**: When you cultivate a good relationship with yourself, you take better care of your physical, emotional, and mental health. This can contribute to improved overall well-being, resilience, and the ability to handle stress and adversity.

3. **Self-confidence and self-esteem**: A healthy relationship with yourself is a key contributor to self-confidence and self-esteem. When you value and respect yourself, it's easier to advocate for your own needs and to pursue the things that fulfil you.

4. **Healthy boundaries**: When you have a solid relationship with yourself, you will establish and maintain healthy boundaries in your relationships with others. This can lead to more satisfying and fulfilling connections with others in personal and business interactions.

5. **Influence on other relationships**: How you treat yourself often reflects on how you treat others. If you are critical and harsh to yourself, you may be the same way with others. On the other hand, if you show kindness, understanding, and patience to yourself, you're likely to express these traits in your relationships as well.

6. **Independence**: A strong relationship with yourself gives you the confidence and capability to be comfortable on your own. While relationships with others are important, it's healthy and empowering to be able to enjoy your own company and rely on yourself. Being comfortable with solitude is an empowering process.

7. **Personal happiness and satisfaction**: Your personal happiness and satisfaction are largely determined by how you view and treat yourself. Having a positive relationship with yourself can lead to higher levels of happiness, satisfaction, and fulfilment in life.

8. **Capacity to cope with hardships**: In times of crisis or hardship, the relationship you have with yourself is often your primary source of strength and resilience. Being able to rely on yourself and treat yourself with compassion during difficult times can be immensely helpful.

Being in an Unhealthy Relationship with Yourself

If you have an unhealthy relationship with yourself, as many do, it reverberates through your interactions with others in various harmful ways. For instance, lower self-esteem and self-confidence can make you feel unworthy or cause a fear of rejection, which might discourage you from social situations or forming close connections. It may also enable you to stay in relationships that are not good for you.

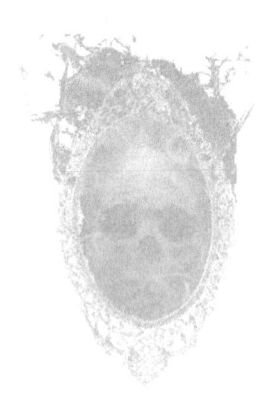

Not valuing yourself can lead to difficulties in setting and maintaining boundaries, which permit others to treat you poorly or to overextend yourself to gain approval. This behaviour can create resentment and potentially damage relationships and yourself.

A negative self-view can lead to increased negativity and criticism towards others, thereby straining interactions. Trust issues can also arise from constant self-doubt and self-criticism, creating conflict, miscommunication, and emotional distance in relationships.

A poor self-relationship can make you overly reliant on others for validation, creating an unhealthy dynamic in which your self-worth is tied to the approval of others, a situation that can result in co-dependency.

Lastly, you might find it difficult to engage fully in relationships if you are too preoccupied with your perceived flaws and insecurities, missing opportunities for meaningful connections.

All these factors make it harder to build and maintain healthy relationships and a healthy career and business, emphasising the importance of treating yourself with respect as the foundation of all other relationships.

Which one sounds most like you?

- Do you have a great personal relationship? or
- Do you have a poor personal relationship?

Remember: You have the power to shape your life and become the best version of yourself. Embrace self-love, embrace your uniqueness, and thrive.

CHAPTER 3:
The Concept of Blueprint

Your blueprint is your thumbprint, as it is unique only to you. Every single person's blueprint will be different, as it will be based on their own personal circumstances and their goals for the future. Since the blueprints for your life and wealth are deeply rooted, it is important that you spend some time carefully considering what you need to include in your own blueprint for an improved, successful, and fulfilled life.

In creating your personal blueprint for *Wealth Beyond Money*, consider carefully your options and what you want in your *designed* blueprint. What do you want it to be, and how do you truly want to spend the rest of your mortal life on this planet? Creating your unique blueprint for your life will enable your unconscious to work in harmony with your conscious to support and challenge you to achieve your mission, vision, and goals.

To help you do this, we will now look at different types of blueprints, myths about these plans for your life, questions that you can ask yourself to help you create a new blueprint for your life, and tips on how to condition your mind for success.

Nature Versus Nurture

Let's first discuss the age-old debate on nature versus nurture and the extent to which certain aspects of our behaviour are caused either by traits we have inherited (nature or genetic) or acquired (nurture or learned) influences.

Nature is everything that is impacted by biological factors or your genetics, which can include health conditions or specific genetic traits that your parents may have that you have also adopted without making any conscious decision to act in that way.

Nurture, on the other hand, refers to influences from external factors, including life experiences and specific things that you have been exposed to after birth that have influenced your behaviour.

It is important not to dismiss either of the thought processes but rather to understand how both ideals work together and combine to create the beings we are. You have the power to change any aspect of your life, whether by nature or nurture, to become the person you want to be and live the life you desire. You do not have to remain who you were born or taught to be. Your Blueprint can be modified with new habits, programming, information, and knowledge to facilitate your journey to become the newly designed future you.

If you were born poor, you don't have to remain poor for the rest of your life. Similarly, if you were born with a condition that affects your ability to achieve academically at school, you do not have to let that keep you from striving for success. Albert Einstein and Stephen Hawking, famous theoretical physicists, and Richard Branson, billionaire and business magnate, all have dyslexia, whereas Elon Musk, entrepreneur and billionaire, Charles Darwin, biologist and geologist, and Bill Gates, co-founder of Microsoft, all have autism spectrum disorder.

Let's look at some more examples. Lionel Messi, arguably one of the best football players in the world, was diagnosed with a growth hormone disorder at the age of 11 (Credihealth, 2023). To treat this, he had to get injections regularly, which severely affected his family's finances. Instead of letting this deter him from continuing to play his favourite sport, he excelled and became one of the highest-paid football stars in history.

Another example is the former president of the United States, Franklin D. Roosevelt. After becoming ill with polio, Roosevelt became almost completely paralysed (*Franklin D. Roosevelt - the First Term*, 2020). He could have allowed this illness to defeat him and stop him from reaching his political dreams, but he didn't and served his country as the first citizen for 12 years.

These famous examples are proof that you can overcome anything life throws at you. What you need is determination and perseverance to succeed, as well as a blueprint to bring you closer to achieving the success you desire.

They could all have allowed their conditions to keep them from reaching their goals, but they chose to rise above them, and maybe the conditions acted as their superpower.

Types of Blueprints

Your genetics should never be used as a crutch or excuse to not reach your goals or achieve *Wealth Beyond Money*. Regardless of your genetics, you will have to make a choice and then decide that you want to rise above any challenges you may face to live the life you want. To do this, you will create a blueprint according to how you want to live your life. The following are different types of blueprints you may want to create for your life.

Basic Life Blueprint

This is a general blueprint for your life that encompasses all the different aspects of it. It is the blueprint that defines the kind of life you are going to have. It determines what decisions you will make, what kind of friendships you want to create, the success you will strive to achieve, the goals you will set, how you will react to failures, how you will learn from your mistakes, and how you will divide your time effectively.

Think about what you want to achieve in your life and what basic steps you need to take to achieve your goals.

Self-Image Blueprint

Your self-image blueprint will be in direct relation to your identity and how you qualify yourself; it is your sense of self and your place in the world. It is, as all blueprints are, shaped by your experiences, cultural influences, and society. It includes how you personally think and feel about yourself and includes your self-esteem, self-worth, self-confidence, values, and beliefs.

The self-image blueprint provides a framework for how you see yourself, how you view your strengths and weaknesses, and what you believe you can achieve. It will influence how you approach challenges and opportunities in your life and how you interact with others. As we have mentioned, your relationship with yourself is crucial to creating *Wealth Beyond Money*. Think about how you currently see yourself. Do you love and respect yourself? Are you happy with the type of person you are? What do you bring to your relationship with yourself? What do other people value about you? What do you value about yourself? What difference can you make in the lives of those around you?

Spend some time to really consider your answers to these questions. This will help you determine if the self-image blueprint, you're currently following is sufficient and will bring you the relationship with yourself that you want. If it will not, you will need to make changes to this blueprint to bring you closer to your goals.

By understanding the links between identity and the self-image blueprint, you can develop a greater sense of self-awareness and work towards creating a more positive and empowering self-image.

Health Blueprint

Your health blueprint is all about the decisions you make to control your good health and prevent poor health. For the majority of you, good health is your start in life, and then life happens, and we lose focus and are influenced into not-so-good compounding habits.

Dr Daniel E. Lieberman, a Harvard Professor, indicates that 75% of diseases are preventable. Please let that sink in. If 75% is preventable, that means 75% of all disease does not need to be!

> *Remember*: Prevention is better than cure and far easier to do and experience

There are many factors that can influence your risk of developing certain conditions, both hereditary and through personal choice. While genetics do play a role in determining your health outcomes, your lifestyle choices and mindset also have a significant impact on your overall well-being. It is recognised that stress and negative emotions have an adverse impact on the body and mind, leading to the risk of developing acute or chronic conditions. Doctors may ask for a complete family medical history to determine risk, and that risk, however high, does not have to become a reality.

If one of your parents has a hereditary illness, it's true that your risk of developing the same condition may be higher. However, this doesn't mean that you are doomed to suffer the same fate. By making conscious choices to live a healthier lifestyle, you can take control of your health and create a new blueprint for your future.

Eating a nutritious diet, engaging in regular exercise, and prioritising proper rest are all key components of a healthy lifestyle that can help reduce your risk of developing hereditary conditions. Additionally, creating a placebo mindset and focusing on your unconscious can also have a powerful impact on your health outcomes.

When considering your health blueprint, it's important to take into account not only your genetics but also your personal lifestyle choices and placebo mindset. By being proactive and taking steps to improve your health, you can break the cycle of hereditary illness and create a new path for your future. Take a moment to reflect on your own health and that of your family members and consider what steps you can take to ensure that you live a healthy, vibrant life.

Relationship Blueprint

The basis of your relationship blueprint is a set of beliefs, values, and expectations that you hold about what you want and need in a relationship. Your blueprint is shaped by your past experiences, upbringing, cultural influences, and personal preferences in relation to any relationship you enter, including friendships, intimate relationships, and business relationships. Your blueprint provides you with a framework to navigate your relationships and cultivate fulfilling relationships. It's important to consider not only your relationships with others but also your relationship with yourself. Loving and accepting yourself has a profound impact on the quality of your relationships with others.

Your personal blueprint includes your preferences linked to communication style, emotional intimacy, trust, shared values, how to express affection and what that means, resolving conflicts and compatibility, and many more.

Consider the relationships you grew up with and the role models you had as a child; did they provide you with a good or poor example? Remember that without external influence, growth, and awareness, your childhood blueprint becomes your *normal*. What lessons can you learn from these relationships to help you improve them in the present and in the future? What have you learned from past relationships about things you definitely do not want in your future relationships?

Think about your current relationships in your life. Are they fulfilling? Where are your current relationships lacking, and what are they missing? What do you really want for the future? What can you do to improve your relationship with yourself and others going forward so that you can get closer to your relationship goals?

Your blueprint is not fixed, and it evolves over time as you gain new experiences and insights. By understanding the various factors that contribute to your relationship blueprint, you can gain greater self-awareness and create more fulfilling and healthy relationships in any aspect of your life. However, if you want different relationships in the future, you can choose to create your own blueprint for relationships to ensure you create the connections you want to have in the future.

Career Blueprint

This blueprint is all about your plans and hopes for the type of career you want to have. This can include wanting to become a manager or the CEO of your company or simply being happy with having a secure job that pays well enough for you to live comfortably. It can also be to be self-employed, to become an entrepreneur, or to do something that makes a difference in others' lives. Everything you do is a choice, and you can create a lifestyle or build a conglomerate. It is your choice between reality and the truth.

It can be that you decide to follow your family's career blueprint or create your own. For example, if you come from a family filled with teachers, you may decide to become an educator as well. Or, you may have a negative impression of the profession and then decide to choose a completely different type of career.

What would you like to achieve in your career, and how do you plan to get there? What steps will you need to take to make your career goals a reality?

Money Blueprint

Your money blueprint is all about your relationship with money, and that behaviour would have been learned from your guardians and their association with money. This blueprint will influence your spending habits and your ability to plan your financial future. A very simple measure of your blueprint is to look at your bank account. Do you save or invest your money, or are you a spender with very little money in the bank or in savings? Do you invest monthly for your future? Do you have savings for any unforeseen events? Do you live beyond your means? Does your money run out before the end of the month?

What would you like your financial health to look like? What new habits can you develop to improve your financial situation and raise your financial IQ? How important are money and the freedom of choice that it can give you? Do you see money as the root of evil, or do you have a healthy relationship with money? Your money blueprint tells you everything you need to know about your relationship and behaviour with money.

If you are currently living above your means, which the vast majority of people do, have you looked at and assessed where you are spending your hard-earned money so that you can change your spending habits in order to start saving money every month? What other skills do you have so that you can earn more money? What changes in your beliefs and mindset can you adopt to create a positive relationship with money? Once you start to make these small changes, you can then start to make your money work hard for you instead of you working hard for it.

Myths of a Blueprint

Before we assist you in creating your own personalised blueprints, let's first look at some misconceptions about these plans for your life and why you should not allow these myths to stand in your way of creating the future you desire.

Universal Blueprints

Every person has a different view of the world and wealth, and your blueprint is adjusted accordingly to your views and plans for the future. The way you see the world is also influenced by your background, upbringing, education, values and beliefs, mass media, cultural norms, and society in general. There is no such thing as a universal blueprint that will help you ensure you reach the success you desire. Your blueprint is as unique to you as your fingerprints; you are unique as is your blueprint.

Apart from designing your own blueprints, blueprints grow and evolve and require evaluation and review frequently. The world is constantly changing, and as a result, the way you go about achieving success will need to be adapted accordingly. Designing your own personal set of blueprints will always stand you in good stead, as they are your uniqueness.

Invisible Script

An invisible script is an underlying belief or assumption that guides your behaviour and decision-making, often without conscious awareness. Invisible scripts can be positive or negative, and they can either empower or limit your potential. Unfortunately, many people live their lives according to invisible scripts that they have either created unconsciously or adopted according to popular beliefs, upbringing, influence, or mass media influence. This includes beliefs that the more money you have, the happier you will be; if you do not endure some pain, you will not get any gains; and spending a lot of money on a gift indicates you care about someone. A positive invisible script may be "hard work pays off," while a negative one may be "you can't trust anyone." The list is almost endless. Identifying and challenging invisible scripts can help you become more aware of your beliefs and biases, allowing you to make more conscious choices and live a more fulfilling life.

While these invisible scripts may not always be wrong, you should be careful when building your blueprint according to them. This is because living your life according to an undesigned blueprint can limit your ability to reach your goals and achieve the *Wealth Beyond Money* you desire. Let's look at the assumption that money brings you happiness. While it is true that having financial wealth makes your life easier, if you have not worked on your relationships with others, you will not have anyone to share your life and experiences with. Instead, work on adapting the invisible scripts in your life according to your aspirations.

Like Father, Like Son—Like Mother, Like Daughter

Many people believe that their life and career choices are limited by what their parents do. If your father is a bus driver, civil servant, or business owner, you will also have to become one, or if your mother is a teacher, doctor, or investment banker, you will also have to follow in her footsteps. This belief can prevent you from striving for the life you want.

There is absolutely no reason why you should follow your parents' career path and life choices if you prefer to do something different in any area of your life.

Similarly, if you grew up poor, you do not have to resolve to stay poor for the rest of your life. You can break free from any shackles that have been holding you back. No matter what your background is, you can achieve the success you want. All you need to do is be willing to educate yourself and work for what you want. It is absolutely 100% possible.

Another misplaced belief that many people have is that they can have great relationships and good health despite working long hours and not exercising. This is simply not realistic or achievable. If you want to create true *Wealth Beyond Money*, you need to find balance in how you spend your energy and your time. Great relationships take time, energy, and effort; good health takes time, attention, and effort; and without them, you will not have the balance and power of the three in harmony.

> **Remember**: *Wealth Beyond Money* is creating balance in life.

CHAPTER 4:
Understanding How Your Blueprint Is Formed

No matter who you are, where you're from, or how old you are, you can change your life. It can only start from here and now. Everything you have done in the past has led you to now and now is not your future. If you are unhappy with where you are, it is time to change. You can take control of your life and create the future you want. It is time to shed the old habits, beliefs, and attitudes holding you back and step boldly into the life you deserve and design. Take action, design your dream lifestyle, and unleash your full potential.

> *Remember*: The power to do so lies within you; no one can change for you.

Every one of you will have a different set of blueprints; you may think you are similar, but in reality, you are not. Your birth, your upbringing, your education, your place of origin, your religious beliefs, your experiences, and your career and business to date all forge a unique set of circumstances that make you "you".

You are born into the world, and then you are influenced by whatever and whoever is around you.

Every situation will impact you and create the beliefs you hold today and the habits that drive your behaviour—some of who you are you will consciously understand, and other parts of you are so deeply ingrained and unconscious you will not understand.

You will do something unconsciously, and when you are aware enough, you will be curious to find out why and either keep the *thing*, tweak the *thing*, or stop the *thing*. Now, you will have to establish what those *things* are for you.

Stages of Life

Each stage of life provides valuable learning that impacts your future, whether you realise it or not. The relationships you were exposed to as a child will be a determining factor in the relationships you seek out in your life. The way your role models handle money will impact your financial health in the future. The lifestyle choices you were exposed to play a role in the health choices you make.

Ages 1–7 are the primary life years that affect you throughout life, trauma or not. They play the biggest part in who you become and believe us; you do not have to remain who you currently are. It is entirely your choice.

Let's look at the different life stages and the various lessons each one brings and remember that you are unique. The lesson you learned may not be the lesson your sibling, friend, or colleague learned, even with similar experiences:

- **Infancy (0-2 years)**: You experience rapid physical development and the beginning of motor skills and language development. The first lessons that shape you, and you have no control over the lessons you receive, are determined by what your caretakers expose you to and form the foundation of the future you will have. We start learning from the moment of conception; we hear and learn while in the womb, and it can affect us for the remainder of our life.

What lessons did you learn during this period of your life? And what influence do they have on you now?

- **Preschool and middle childhood (2-6 years)**: The wider world starts to open up, and this stage is marked by the development of independence, the start of education, and significant social and emotional development. You are still heavily influenced by your caregivers. Are they promoting independence or dependence? Are they loving and nurturing or hateful and hurtful? What is their influence over who you become? This is a vital period for childhood development that stays with you long into adulthood. Whatever your early lessons, remember they can be healed, and you are magical and your own gold.

What lessons did you learn during this period of your life? And what influence do they have on you now?

- **Late childhood (7-11 years)**: In this stage, you improve your skills in various areas, such as problem-solving, comprehension, and social interaction, while also beginning to form a more complex understanding of the world. You become more self-aware and experience building relationships outside of the family, which may last you a lifetime or not. Your interactions become important, and you start to see results, resulting in cognitive development. You learn the basic skills of life, which are vital for your future. Learned behaviour can be unlearned later, if necessary.

What lessons did you learn during this period of your life? And what influence do they have on you now?

- **Adolescence (12-18 years of age)**: This is typically a turbulent time in your life; you experience rapid physical changes and the development of a stronger individual identity, along with the start of deeper emotional and intellectual capacities. You no longer feel and behave like a child and are not emotionally ready for adulthood yet. During this time, making social connections is important, and you learn from friends. This is also the period where potential peer pressure escalates. Do you join in, skirt around the edges, or leave and stand alone?

What lessons did you learn during this period of your life? And what influence do they have on you now?

- **Young adulthood (19-40 years of age)**: Typically characterised by building the foundation for your romantic, social, professional, and financial future. The main conflict during this stage is between isolation and intimacy. You may deeply want to experience love and connection with others, but you may also fear failing and disappointment, which will result in you isolating yourself. If you grew up with examples of unhealthy relationships, this stage can be even more challenging for you. Start by focusing on one connection and gradually increase your connections as your confidence increases.

What lessons did you learn during this period of your life? And what influence do they have on you now?

- **Middle adulthood (40–60 years)**: During this phase, your foundation may be solid because you have focused on career, business, and life development, and you reap the rewards of your foresight, planning, and efforts. However, this is typically when you discover that you are not on the right path to gaining your desired success. If this is the case, create a new vision, set new goals, and ensure you follow the correct plans to get you closer to reaching them.

What lessons did you learn during this period of your life? And what influence do they have on you now? What do you need to unlearn to relearn the new?

- **Late adulthood (60+ for some)**: This may involve retirement, lifestyle changes, dealing with health-related issues, and reflecting on life. For many others, this is their time to reap the rewards of a life well-planned and executed. You have health, a beautiful relationship, and money to spend. After all, we have heard that 60 is the new 40! What we want to say here is that it is never too late to renew, refresh, and reinvigorate. This stage of life is characterised by introspection and reflection. Many of you will be on the path of sharing your life wisdom with others.

Regardless of physical age, life has changed, and the world is not what it once was. The young teach the old, and the older share their life wisdom; both learn from each other.

Adopt a new model of the world: the old do not have to be sick, and the young do not have to be wisdom less. Increase your opportunities to reach the success you desire, accept lessons from others, listen well, and adopt the strategies in your life regardless of your current age—after all; it is just a number for you to believe or reject:

- Uncover and resolve any trauma you may have. Emotions run deep and affect your values and beliefs, both limiting and enabling you. Logically, you may have dealt with it, and emotionally, it carries weight. If you feel something is blocking you, talk to someone who is professional and knows what to do.
- Create a personal development plan covering the areas you want to focus on—self-mastery is a delight; attach it to your vision, and success is yours for the taking.
- Self-awareness is the key to self-mastery. Learn who you are, identify your patterns and drivers, and work with them or change them—the world is your oyster with wisdom, foresight, and hindsight.
- Identify areas of your life you need to improve and make it happen—you can.
- Commit, design, and take action to make the necessary changes you have decided upon. Change your thinking, change your actions, and change your life; it is a recipe for your success.

> *Remember*: As you confidently embark on refining the multifaceted elements of you and your life, forged through the various life stages, the smoother the process of instigating change becomes, taking you closer to your vision.

Choose to perceive your life as a journey of self-discovery, where you are consistently on the lookout for opportunities to enhance your existence. Your past does not dictate your future unless you allow it to—it is your resolve to change and the choices you make today that shape your tomorrow.

Identity and Ego

The ego is only an illusion, but a very influential one. Letting the ego-illusion become your identity can prevent you from knowing your true self.

—Wayne Dyer

We all have an identity that we live by, and we all have an ego that drives us—knowing and understanding is the first stage in understanding that who we think we are is not who we have to remain, and some of who we are is exactly what we need to remain and build on, and some is not.

The identity of a human being, you, is complex and is created and evolves through your lifetime, shaped by all of your experiences, interactions, and learning processes.

You are a person, and who you are has been shaped by everything that has happened to you in your life stages. When you were a baby, you learned who you were from the way people cared for you. As a child, your family and friends influenced you, and you started forming your own ideas and feelings about yourself. When you were a teenager, you started to look for your own path. You tried new things; you may have rebelled or been compliant; you sometimes made mistakes and sometimes succeeded, and that helped you understand yourself better when you thought about and learned from the experience.

As adults, your identity continues to be honed by relationships, career paths, life transitions, and even challenges or crises. Throughout these stages, external factors like culture, religion, socio-economic status, and the environment you create and inhabit play a significant role, as do internal elements such as cognitive development, emotional intelligence, and personality traits.

You will also have realised that where you come from, your traditions and your personal choices play a big role in who you are and form part of your identity.

From these experiences, you will have formed an identity that you may know about or not, and you will have one.

How do you identify yourself, and how does that affect you creating *Wealth Beyond Money*? Does it spur you on or hold you back?

Identity and ego are not the same thing, although they are closely related.

Identity refers to the way we understand and perceive ourselves, and how we believe others see us. It's an evolving construct composed of individual traits, personal history, social roles, and cultural affiliations. Identity encapsulates our beliefs, values, and attitudes. It is about "who I am."

On the other hand, the ego, a term popularised by Sigmund Freud, is a part of the psyche that mediates between the conscious and unconscious minds. The ego and you all have one—never deny that—is a self-regulatory force striving for balance between primitive drives, morals, and social expectations (Raton, 2019).

Freud described it as "the part of the mind that mediates between the conscious and the unconscious and is responsible for reality testing and a sense of personal identity."

In far simpler terms, the ego is like the manager of your personality, making decisions and controlling impulses based on what's practical and socially acceptable to you. It plays a part in forming your identity, but it's not the entirety of your identity.

Who and what is your ego? Does it get in your way or open doors for you?

Values: How Do They Affect Your Results?

What are values? They are essentially the principles and standards of conduct that you deem essential. Yet, recognising these values is not always straightforward. Your values serve as the guidelines dictating your actions, decisions, and interactions with others.

Your values act as your life's driving force. Whether you are aware of them or not, it is vital to identify your values, understand their impacts, and comprehend how they shape your actions and motivations.

Values mirror your perception of right and wrong, good and evil. These beliefs can be shaped by a multitude of factors, such as your cultural background, personal experiences, religious faith, and familial upbringing.

There are over 400 identifiable values, each carrying your unique influence, and it will be your top three to five that have the biggest impact on you and your results. There are values that drive you towards and there are values that drive you away – establishing what they both are, and instilling easy rules to follow will support you in achieving whatever you desire.

Values are not uniformly defined, despite common belief. Take authenticity as an example. We often hear about the importance of authenticity, but what does it truly mean? To what or to whom are you being authentic? This authenticity is largely a product of your upbringing.

Let us provide you with an example: a liar is authentic to lying, a thief is authentic to thieving, a philanthropist is authentic to doing good in their chosen way—the list of examples could be endless, and we trust this has got you thinking about your authenticity.

If you value honesty, your definition of honesty might differ significantly from someone else's interpretation.

Everyone carries a unique background that significantly influences their lives, often beyond their control.

However, when you realise that you can shape your destiny, it sparks a profound moment that could either lead to transformative change or remain just a moment of thought.

Simply put, values serve as a life compass, giving you direction, aiding decision-making, and defining who you are. They mould your attitudes, influence your perceptions, steer your behaviours, and play a fundamental role in forging your identity.

The beauty of values lies in their flexibility. They can be revised, reordered, and better understood as you journey through life.

Make your values conscious, and you will understand why you do what you do.

> **Remember**: Your values will influence the goals you set and your worldview, whether you know it or not, and they will affect your results.

Questions to Help You Assess Your Blueprint

A blueprint is the foundation for everything you create for yourself in life. It is the base you operate from, and as such, it could be like set cement for some, while for others, your blueprint can be fluid and flexible.

The greater your learning, the greater your ability to change your foundation to a more robust personal choice. It helps to revisit and check in to assess and evaluate if your current blueprint is still serving you, and if not, change it. Consider all the aspects we have shared within this book and work for and towards harmony.

The Exercise

Here are a few questions to work through as a starter to assess your current blueprint and design your future blueprint:

Overarching

- What aspects of your blueprint are serving you well, and what areas do you need to work on to reach your goals and live a fulfilling life?

- How do your beliefs and attitudes in the areas of health, relationships, career, mental health, communication, and finance contribute to your overall sense of purpose and fulfilment in life?

- What is your idea of being rich? What does it really mean for you, and how do you think it feels to be rich?

- What effect does the economy have on your life and finances?

- How do you communicate your needs and boundaries effectively, and what steps do you take to maintain healthy relationships?

- What steps are you taking to develop your communication skills and build stronger relationships with others?

- How do you manage everyday life, and what tools do you use to cope with challenging situations?

Self-Relationship

- How do you feel about yourself? What aspects of yourself do you feel you need to work on?

- How do you balance your needs with the needs of others in your relationships?

- What strategies do you use to maintain a positive mindset?

- What is your relationship with self-care, and how do you make time for activities that bring you joy and relaxation?

- How do you handle difficult emotions, such as anger or sadness, and what tools do you use to cope?

Health

- What steps are you taking to address any health concerns or issues that you may have?

- How do you prioritise your mental health?

- What habits do you have that impact your emotional well-being?

- What steps are you taking to address any mental health concerns or issues you may have?

- How do you handle stress, and what strategies do you use to maintain a healthy work-life-love balance?

- What is your relationship with nutritious food, alcohol, and tobacco, and how does this impact your overall health?

- How do you prioritise your physical health, and what habits do you have that impact your well-being?

- How do you approach exercise, and how often do you engage in physical activity?

Nutrition

- Do you drink the minimum daily water consumption for optimum health, which is 8 glasses or 2 litres?

- Do you consume at least 5 servings of fresh fruits and vegetables every day?

- Do you make an effort to avoid processed foods, and if so, how do you achieve this?

- Do you consume less than 2 units a day of alcohol?

- Do you eat, on most days, less than 2000 calories for a woman and 2500 calories for a man?

- How does your relationship with nutritious food, alcohol, and tobacco impact your overall health?

- Are you aware of the significance and importance of eating the correct ratio of Protein, Carbohydrates, and Fat to maintain your healthy target weight?

- What steps do you take to address any deficiencies in your nutrition, such as taking supplements or consulting with the correct professional?

Relationships

- How do you approach communication with others in all relationships, and what patterns do you notice in your interactions?

- How do you approach difficult conversations, and what tools do you use to facilitate productive communication?

- How do you handle conflict or disagreement in your relationships, and what strategies do you use to resolve issues?

- What are your priorities when it comes to relationships, and how do you balance these with other areas of your life?

- Are you happy with the relationships you currently have? What types of relationships are you lacking?

- What do you look for in a romantic partner or friend, and how does this impact your relationships?

- What value do you bring to your relationships?

Career

- What is your attitude when it comes to work? Do you enjoy your work, or do you simply work to pay the bills?

- Are you happy with your chosen career path?

- What can you do to bring you closer to your career goals?

- How do you approach your work, and what motivates you to be productive?

- What are your strengths and weaknesses in the workplace?

- How do you leverage them to achieve success?

- What steps are you taking to develop new skills and knowledge to advance your career?

- What are your current career goals?

- How are you working towards them?

Business

- What is the overall vision and mission statement of your business?

- What are your business objectives and goals for the next year? Do they reflect your current market conditions and competitive landscape?

- How well does your current business address the needs and preferences of your target audience?

- How well-defined and documented are your core business processes?

- What are the business values that you live by?

- If you are thinking of starting a business, what do you need to learn?

Finance

- What are your current financial goals, and how are you working towards them?

- How do you approach spending and saving money, and how does this impact your financial situation?

- What is your attitude towards debt, and how do you manage it?

- How do you feel about money? How do you feel about people who view money in a different way?

- Do you feel comfortable discussing your finances with friends, or do you think talking about money with other people is off-limits?

- How do you feel about your current income level, and what steps can you take to increase your earning potential?

- How do you plan for the future, such as retirement or unexpected expenses?

- Do you follow a conservative approach when it comes to your finances, or are you willing to take some risks?

Assessing and reflecting on various aspects of your life is crucial for personal growth and creating a blueprint for a fulfilling future. By addressing the questions related to health, nutrition, relationships, career, business, and finance, you will gain valuable insights into areas that require improvement and those that already serve you well.

Taking immediate steps to prioritise your mental, emotional, and physical health, including good nutrition, regular exercise, and stress management, can greatly impact your overall well-being.

Exercise: Understanding How Your Blueprint Is Formed

Stop reading or listening to the book and capture your instant feelings and thoughts on the questions. They will tell you a lot about you and how you think and feel about all the areas of your life.

You can come back to this later when you have completed the entire book and, with increased knowledge and thoughts, orchestrate your plan, goals, and path forward.

Proviso: as long as you are somewhere safe—not if you are driving, of course.

Contemplate

- Areas for Improvement
- Areas to start
- Areas to stop
- Areas to continue

Remember: DO NOT beat yourself up. Celebrate your success and recognise that there are probably areas you can improve.

Embrace the opportunity to design a remarkable blueprint for your future, one that encompasses all aspects of your life: health, nutrition, relationships, career, business, and finance.

PLEASE revisit this after you have read or listened to the entire book—there is a reminder at the end.

> **Remember**: Perfection does not exist, so there is no negative comparison, and you can only start from where you are.

CHAPTER 5:
Why Change?

It's not necessary to change, survival is not mandatory.
— W. Edwards Demming

Change Is Constant

You will often hear the phrase "change is constant." This sounds so obvious and so easy, and yet, for many of you, much of the time, you still act as if it is something you can resist, ignore, or prevent.

Change is an inevitable part of life, whether it's something that happens to you or something you choose. Embracing change is important for maintaining balance in your life. When you are open to change, you become better equipped to adapt to new situations and seize new opportunities. Although change can sometimes be challenging, it can be helpful to approach new tasks by focusing on one step at a time.

By taking things one step at a time and celebrating wins along the way, you will be able to navigate change smoothly and maintain your balance.

When you think about growth in life and business, it is imperative that you, as a leader, be an advocate of change. Supporting, challenging, monitoring, and evaluating the change ensures it is embedded in the hearts and souls of you and those around you.

Let us recognise that:

- Some change is imposed
- Some change is chosen
- Some change is small
- Some change is enormous
- Some change is natural evolution
- Some change is revolutionary

Each will have its own consequences and will require implementation differently. Depending on how you got to where you are currently, you may need to make a revolutionary, enormous, and imposed change of choice!

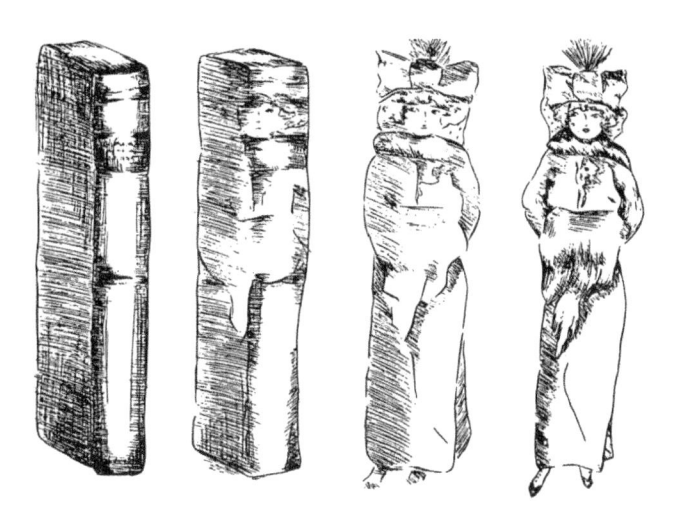

What Stops Change?

Making your chosen changes in your life to bring you closer to the success you desire requires courage, energy, effort, and perseverance. You will grow beyond your current comfort zone, and you will willingly put yourself in a position you may not have been in previously to create your own *Wealth Beyond Money*. Your personal and life self-mastery increases its reach and influence; you become the best version of you version 2, version 3, and version 4 — and it is ongoing; your future is yours to design, activate, and live, and it involves change.

Intriguingly, the process of designing and implementing change can sometimes seem daunting, causing you to pause or stop prior to reaching and sometimes even starting your dreamed of and desired future result.

With increased knowledge and self-awareness, you can confidently break through these limiting barriers, knowing that your capacity to evolve and adapt is one of your greatest strengths. It is in your power as a human being to make cognitive choices about thoughts and behaviours.

> *Remember*: You are your leader; are you leading you well?

Let's explore some of the most frequently encountered reasons why change might initially feel challenging.

- **Personal beliefs and values**: Your life to date, and especially your formative years, has created a set of values that you live by. They formulate your beliefs, which transition through to your habits, feelings, and emotions, resulting in your behaviour. If something is blocking you from achieving your dream, investigate this area of your life. Everything can be worked through to release all obstacles and create personal power and change.

- **Lack of clear goals and vision**: Without a clear understanding of what you want to achieve, initiating and maintaining change will be challenging. What path will you follow without your personal guiding light — your path or someone else's? We are all goal-driven creatures all of the time — make yours consciously visible and own it. Create your own golden thread to counteract any that may be imposed on you.
- **Toxic environment**: If you have been in, or are in a toxic environment, you may feel like you are not worthy of creating the success you desire. This environment can be both personal and professional. If your self-worth and self-esteem are low, you may not think you are capable of breaking free from the shackles that have been holding you back for however long it has been. Believe us, work on this and escape, and you can metamorphose into the strong, powerful, beautiful being you were created to be. Think of pupae becoming butterflies.

- **Traumatic childhood**: If you have experienced trauma in your past, either known or unknown, remembered or not remembered, you may feel like you are incapable of achieving the success you deserve. Your past does not have to equal your future; a condition of being a human being is that you have a choice and can change. You cannot remove the past, but what you can do is remove the emotional baggage it leaves you with, resulting in greater freedom for your future. Now, you may want to hold onto the past as it has created your identity, and that can change as well.
- **Resistance to change**: Pure and simple, you are so comfortable with where you are now, even if you do not like it, that you are unwilling to do anything differently. You are the master and mistress of your destiny, for good and bad. Repeated habits have brought you to where you are now, and do you want to compound those or change them? You may prefer the comfort of familiar routines and environments. Alterations, even for the better, can be met with resistance due to your preference for familiarity. The path is certainty through uncertainty, and certainty once more. The certainty is certainty to your vision and goals.

- **Fear of judgement from others**: When you make changes in your life, others might not understand why you are leaving behind everything you know to follow a new, unfamiliar goal. This may result in others judging you, and this judgement can keep you from going after what you want. Support from friends, family, and professionals can significantly impact one's ability to change. Without it, the path may seem too daunting. 'Crabs' want you to stay in the same bucket, and change builds a new bucket for you to swim in.
- **Fear of failure or success**: Poses a real challenge as you navigate through changes in your life. You step into the unknown, moving away from the familiar, and you might grapple with the fear of faltering in your new endeavours. Such fear can be a formidable obstacle to change, often holding you back from taking the initial step due to the potentially paralysing and overwhelming thought of making a mistake and not achieving success. Linking this to the influence of self-doubt, lack of confidence, and self-criticism, you can realise why you may not change — being aware this may occur is crucial for you to understand.

4. "I wish I had stayed in touch with my friends." As life progresses, people often lose touch with old friends due to various reasons, such as distance or busyness. This regret emphasises the value of creating, nurturing, and maintaining friendships, as they provide support, companionship, and a sense of belonging.

5. "I wish I had let myself be happier." Many individuals realise too late that happiness is a choice and that they could have allowed themselves to experience more joy and contentment. This regret serves as a reminder to prioritise happiness and not get caught up in negative emotions or circumstances. Control and influence what you can, and distance yourself from what you cannot.

These regrets highlight the importance of living with integrity and authenticity, finding balance, expressing emotions, nurturing relationships, and seeking happiness in life. Not one said, *I wish I had more money in the bank*! By reflecting on these regrets, you can strive to make choices aligned with your values and priorities to live a more fulfilling life, creating *Wealth Beyond Money* for yourself and those you love.

What do these regrets mean for you currently and how you live your life?

> ***Remember:*** You can change prior to your deathbed, and the sooner you do, the more life you have to live in joy and *Wealth Beyond Money*.

Problem—Research—Solution

Problems, research, and solutions are interconnected aspects of personal change. Lack of self-awareness hinders progress, while research provides understanding and effective strategies. Solutions involve taking action through goal setting and adopting new habits. The process, without doubt, requires vision, commitment, self-awareness, reflection, and adaptability to overcome your resistors and habits and achieve your desired goals.

You can be in personal conflict with each part of the problem, research, and solution. You may be resistant to acknowledging or accepting the existence of a problem. If you do not recognise or agree that you have a problem, you may dismiss the need for research and a solution altogether, even when it is staring you in the face.

This hinders your personal growth and changes towards *Wealth Beyond Money* as it prevents you from seeking the necessary understanding and taking action to address the underlying issues.

Embracing change is essential for creating the true *Wealth Beyond Money* that you desire in your life. It's important to understand that some changes you can choose and plan for, while others may come unexpectedly. When faced with unexpected changes, it's crucial to remain calm and control your response.

> *Remember*: You always have the power and choice to decide how you want to respond to these changes.

By embracing change and responding positively, you can make a significant difference in your journey towards true wealth.

Change is either imposed or chosen, resisted, or accepted, and there are four main reasons why people change:

- When you hurt enough, you have to.
- When you see something or someone that inspires you to.
- When you learn enough that you want to.
- When you have access to personal resources that enable the process of change.

Think about your life and what your reasons are for wanting to make changes. What drives you to improve the quality of your life? Do you want to give yourself and your family a better life? Are you tired of not having everything that your heart desires? Are you scared of what the future might hold and, therefore, want to create wealth to ensure health freedom, relationship magic, and financial abundance?

Whatever your reasons for wanting to make the necessary changes to your life may be, use them as powerful forces to propel you into securing success in your future. Any form of change is possible when you are motivated enough to want to succeed.

The Change Curve — The Emotional Effect

We know what we are but know not what we may be.
— **William Shakespeare**

Being able to accept and embrace the necessary changes you will make in your life plays a key role in your ability to create the true wealth that you desire. Understanding the power, you hold in deciding how you are going to respond to changes will make a massive difference in your ability to create *Wealth Beyond Money* in all aspects of your life, including your health, relationships, and finances.

When you face changes in your life, you will likely experience a host of different emotions that not only help you understand the importance of making these changes but also motivate you to do whatever is necessary to ensure these changes will bring the desired results. To help you understand these emotions and why it will be helpful to experience and accept each of them fully in order to make lasting changes in your life, we will look at the Change Curve, which is based on research that was originally developed in the 1960s by Dr Elisabeth Kubler-Ross.

The original research was conducted on the terminally ill, and through interviews and observations, Dr Kubler-Ross identified five stages of emotional change that were common experiences: Denial, Anger, Bargaining, Depression, and Acceptance. Of course, with all the great pieces of research and work, the model is adapted and expanded into everyday life and business change and is a useful model for personal change.

The following description is tailored to encompass change through choice rather than being tied to terminal illness. It elaborates on the diverse range of emotions you are likely to encounter when confronting any form of change, whether it be through personal choice or external circumstances.

When faced with change, a myriad of emotions can arise. Initially, there may be excitement and anticipation as the prospect of something new and different unfolds before you. The thrill of venturing into the unknown can be invigorating, bringing a sense of adventure and possibility. Change disrupts your comfort zone and challenges familiar routines, which may trigger a sense of unease and uncertainty. Doubts may surface, and you might question your abilities to navigate the unfamiliar path ahead.

Change rarely follows a straight path, and obstacles or unforeseen challenges may arise. These moments can test your resilience. However, they also provide opportunities for growth and learning as you discover new strategies and develop greater adaptability.

It is important to acknowledge and accept the emotions you experience as natural responses to your evolution. Embracing change requires emotional resilience and self-compassion, allowing yourself to feel and process these emotions while remaining open to the transformative potential they bring.

By recognising and embracing the diverse emotions that accompany change, you can travel the path ahead with greater understanding, resilience, and purpose:

Denial: In the first stage, individuals often respond to change with shock, which is quickly followed by denial; the two emotions can occur almost simultaneously. You may find it challenging to accept or comprehend the change, even when you have chosen it and say you want it. You may even deny its existence and carry on exactly as before. This can be a defence mechanism to protect yourself from the emotional impact of the change.

For example, if the change is a company restructuring and you accept the offer of redundancy, on the last day of service, you may carry on working as normal as though nothing was going to change — one of the authors has witnessed this personally. If it is a personal change linked to a health condition, you refuse to accept the diagnosis and the necessary lifestyle changes. You downplay the severity of the condition and seek alternative explanations to avoid facing the emotional impact of the health change.

You do not believe the situation you are in will affect you and that you do not have to make any changes. You may even search for any evidence that what you can clearly see is not true.

Anger: As the reality of the change begins to sink in, individuals may experience anger and frustration. Once you realise that your life will be impacted by the situation and that change is inevitable, you can rebel against your own personal choice as well, and when the anger and frustration at yourself turn inward without relief, it is dangerous to your health.

You might feel a sense of injustice or resentment towards those responsible for the change or the circumstances surrounding it. In the case of the company's restructuring, you may direct your anger towards management or the economic conditions that led to the decision.

Linked to the health change, whether it be choice or imposed, you may feel resentful towards your own body, blaming it for betraying you. Or you direct anger towards the healthcare system, believing it failed to prevent or detect this condition earlier.

> **Remember**: For the majority of you, your health condition is of your own making! It's harsh for some to read and true.

You resent having to make lifestyle changes, significant or minor, feeling that life is now unfair and burdened with restrictions.

Your anger and frustration serve as manifestations of your struggle to accept the reality of living with the health condition and the adjustments it demands from you.

You may feel upset that you're forced to make certain changes, especially when you don't actually want to implement them, even though you chose them!

Bargaining: In this stage, you may attempt to negotiate with yourself or others in an effort to regain some control or reverse the change. You may seek alternatives or propose compromises.

For instance, employees facing the company restructuring may attempt to negotiate for different roles, reduced hours, or other arrangements they believe will mitigate the impact of the change.

With health, you may start to look for alternative treatments, researching options in an attempt to find a way to reverse or mitigate the condition's impact.

You may negotiate with health professionals, requesting additional tests or treatments you believe offer better outcomes.

You may make personal promises or changes in hopes of striking a deal with fate, such as adopting a strict diet or lifestyle modifications.

When you engage in bargaining, it allows you to feel a sense of control and actively participate in your healthcare decisions, seeking to find a way to improve and regain your health.

Bargaining provides an opportunity to influence and regain control where you can. It is part of the process of letting go and moving forward.

Depression: As individuals, when you begin to accept the reality of the situation and the limitations of your ability to control it, you may experience feelings of sadness, grief, and hopelessness, which can affect your ability to think clearly and make decisions and can also result in you lacking the energy to follow through with any decisions you do make.

As the bargaining stage proves ineffective, as it does with imposed change that you cannot control or influence. You may start to experience a sense of helplessness and potentially be overwhelmed by the reality of the change and the challenges it presents. In the context of the company restructuring, you may feel a deep sense of loss for your colleagues who are let go, fear for your own job security, and an unknown about the changing dynamics within the organisation.

This phase is characterised by a general lack of motivation and confusion. You may be uncertain as to what the future holds and how you fit into the future "world". Your core sense of self may be affected, which can leave you adrift with little sense of identity and no clear vision of how to operate or what to do next.

Now here is a thought: The negotiation stage fails with yourself, or you succeed and move forward with the change. This stage of depression can take you out; it is easy to give up, and this is the stage for perseverance and keeping the vision in sight. Change as a general concept is not a smooth curve; you will ebb and flow from one stage to the next. When you truly want the change, you are creating, this stage does not get deep; you do not become depressed; you can short-circuit and expect the feeling of letting go of one thing to move on to the next—the process is perfectly normal.

Acceptance: In the final stage, you come to terms with the change and accept its reality. You adapt and adjust your mindset and behaviours accordingly. You understand that there is no going back. You start to create and become the new you, whatever that is required to be. You may be forging a new identity to take you into your new future.

In the case of the company restructuring, you accept the new organisational structure, focus on developing new skills, and explore new opportunities and a new culture. With the health example, you experiment with how to do a new *'thing'*. You do things differently.

At this stage, it is common to make mistakes. Be prepared, and it is perfectly normal that you are doing something you have not done before. You try out your new ways of thinking and acting. You experiment with the new situation, the new way, and the new process.

The final stage of the process of change is:

Integration: In this final stage of change, you have accepted the changes you have chosen to make or have had imposed on you and trust your decision that these changes will benefit you — the choice is conscious.

This transformation requires a conscious effort to adapt and incorporate the change seamlessly into daily routines, creating new habits. Initially, this may feel 'clunky' as you navigate unfamiliar territory. However, with perseverance and consistency, you begin to develop new habits that support the change.

This may involve establishing a structured schedule, setting reminders or cues, and practising repetition to reinforce the desired behaviour. Over time, the change becomes integrated into your everyday life, and what was once unfamiliar becomes second nature. As new habits take root, you find yourself more comfortable and adept at managing the change, allowing you to thrive in your transformed reality.

> ***Remember***: Change is constant, and the more you do it, the easier it becomes.

The Benefits of Change

> *It is not the strongest of the species that survives,*
> *nor the most intelligent that survives,*
> *it is the one that is most adaptable to change.*
>
> –Charles Darwin

While many people choose to stay in their comfort zones and avoid making the necessary changes to create *Wealth Beyond Money*, it is important that you choose the correct mindset to embrace the changes that are necessary to have an improved, successful, and fulfilling life. Let's look at some of the benefits you will acquire when you learn to choose and embrace change:

- **Flexibility and creativity**: When you try new things, challenge yourself, and embrace change, you will be far more adaptable and calmer in all environments and situations.

- **New opportunities**: When you are willing to take risks, make considered changes, and try new things, you open yourself up to new opportunities that you may not have otherwise encountered. This includes new relationships, increased health and vitality, career and business opportunities, personal experiences, and financial acumen.

- **New beginnings**: Change is inevitable in life; after all, it is one of the main constants; evolution does not stop. The more you step into the new you, which is outside of your current comfort zone, the better equipped you become to handle anything and everything. You are the architect and designer of your life.

- **Personal growth**: Stepping outside your comfort zone and into change will help you develop new skills and learn more about yourself. It will also help you build confidence, courage, and resilience; you will learn from the experiences and develop into the new you, overcoming obstacles that have previously held you back.

- **Progress**: All changes will bring progress to your life. Even when a change you make does not bring the desired results, it will bring with it valuable learning, which will lead you to make better choices and changes in the future. Even if you don't make the progress, you might have wanted, you will still make progress as these changes will bring new opportunities.

- **The snowball effect**: This is where you focus on one small change at a time, 1% daily. This is linked to your mission, vision, and goals, which are linked to enhancing your health, relationships, and financial situation, creating *Wealth Beyond Money*. These small, incremental changes have an impact that cannot be underestimated. This is by far the easiest way to condition yourself and your mind.

Armed with insight into how transformational change can be and now equipped with the strategy to implement it productively, it is exciting to remember that change is not only good but also manageable and within your reach.

Remember: Harness the power of change in all its glory because you can absolutely do it!

CHAPTER 6:
How to Change

---

*Embrace change and adaptability; they are the keys
to staying ahead in a fast-paced world.*

–Julie Hogbin

To make lasting changes, behave deliberately. Actively work towards your goals and create new habits that support your vision. Be conscious of your decisions and actions, and do not let your old habits and beliefs hold you back. It may, at times, be challenging, but keep pushing forward towards the life you deserve. Take control of your life, be deliberate and conscious in your actions, and create the change you want to see.

Setting your goals according to your own timeline is crucial to achieving the success you desire. It is important to be aware of changes in the world—from shifts in the economy to changes in social dynamics, relationships, family circumstances, and your networks — and to be adaptable in the face of these changes. You are constantly evolving and growing, and your goals will reflect that. Guide yourself to a life of wealth and abundance beyond just monetary success. Do not hold back; create and step into the new you and the new future and stage of life.

Reprogramming Your Mind

Don't get so busy making a living that you forget to make a life.

–Dolly Parton

Understanding what changes, you want or need to make is the first step in improving your future and creating *Wealth Beyond Money*. However, this will be pointless if you do not work on creating a successful mindset to support and challenge yourself to effectively implement the changes. To do this, understand that you need to choose to see the good in everything that happens to you, there will be a reason for it somewhere, and be able to turn all experiences into positive learning.

This empowers your unconscious mind for success through focused habitual decision-making, which bypasses the need to analyse actions and make decisions through your conscious mind. Consider an example of how your unconscious and conscious minds collaborate: Initially, your conscious mind decides to acquire a new skill and learns the necessary steps. With practice, the skill becomes second nature, allowing your unconscious mind to take over effortlessly.

> *Remember*: The new way becomes your new habit with commitment and consistency.

Reprogramming your unconscious is creating new habits; it is how the unconscious is programmed, both intentionally and unintentionally. Much of what you currently do is an unintentional habit you have formed through your experiences; now is the time to examine and reprogram yourself to achieve what you desire.

According to research, new habits take between 16 and 254 days to embed, with a mean of 66 days. Habits are things you repeatedly do, often without thinking. Make your repeated processes those you wish for— it is your choice for your future — and design them well.

Your unconscious is always in play and, believe it or not, in charge of what you do and how you do it. Once you accept this to be true, your future is entirely in your control:

- **Decide**: Take charge and clearly define the transformative changes you desire in your life. Reflect on your goals and envision how these changes will enrich your journey, fuelling you towards your vision. As you deepen your comprehension of your choices and grasp the profound value these changes bring, you pave the way for implementation. By consciously mapping your decisions, you unlock your unconscious mind's innate support and limitless potential, which steadfastly guide you along your chosen path. Be prepared. It can be the ride of a lifetime.

- **Commit**: Once you've determined the transformations you wish to introduce into your life, it's time to activate those plans. Embracing this step with enthusiasm, dedication, and perseverance is crucial for you and your future. Let your vision for success and balance propel you forward. Embrace the challenges that come along and treat each one as a stepping stone to the new you, the new way, and the life you have designed. Follow your new belief system and process and access your courage and heart to accept the new learnings and change.

- **Resolve**: Navigating the path forward when faced with conflicting options requires steadfast resolve. This resolve comes from the courage to make informed decisions, fuelled by a clear understanding of your values and long-term goals. It's about remaining adaptable, resilient, and committed, viewing each conflicting route as an opportunity for growth and understanding. Trust in your intuition and the new wisdom you've gained. Remember, it's not about choosing the easiest path but the one that aligns with your personal and professional aspirations, promising the most rewarding journey.

Once you reprogram your unconscious to the new way, the new you, and your designed future. You create true personal power and place yourself on the road to reaching your goals. You will view everything as a learning opportunity, and you will utilise every opportunity that leads you towards your new life.

> **Remember**: Your habits are created consciously or unconsciously and drive your every action.

The following points are for you to acknowledge some of the changes required:

- **Develop enabling beliefs**: Believe in yourself and know you are worthy. Adopt positive self-talk, create, and utilise affirmations and afformations. Work towards success by thinking for yourself and dealing with any limiting beliefs you may have. Remember, we are born with only two fears: falling and loud noises. Therefore, anything else has been made up by you for you and, therefore, can be unmade and changed.

- **Focus on positive action**: Know what you need to do and when you need to do it. Focus on areas you can control primarily and influence secondary — do not spend time in the no-control zone. Use your energy, time, and effort wisely every step of the way towards your vision. Prioritise your actions and celebrate wins along the way. Success is a powerful process for feeling good and knowing you can.

- **Be grateful**: Gratitude is one of the most powerful forces in the universe. When real gratitude is expressed, it is heard, and when you are truly grateful, it creates abundance. There is magic within this equation, without a doubt. Simply put, if you are not grateful, why would anyone or anything give you more? Give without expectation of receiving, and eventually, what you receive will fulfil your visualised desire.

- **Increase positive influences**: Create a positive environment for yourself in all you do. Friends, family, and networks design it all to support you in creating your *Wealth Beyond Money*. Energies are contagious, both positive and negative—ensure you gain as much of the positive as you can. If it means cutting out the negative, make it happen. Time is precious, and so are you.

> *Remember*: Embrace the power of self-education and unlock new opportunities and possibilities in your life.

Vision Leads to Focus

If you always do what you have always done, you will always get what you have always got.

- Henry Ford

Without a clear vision, what are you focusing on? Having a clear vision will give you the *focus* you need to achieve your outcome. *Vision* and *Focus* are critical elements in achieving success in any aspect of your life. Your mind is an incredible tool that will either accelerate or sabotage your journey towards achieving your goals. If you are not in control of your mind, it will control you, and it is very possible that you end up in a place you do not want to be.

Focusing requires training your mind to concentrate on what matters most to you and how to reach your desired destination in a more efficient and beneficial way. It will enable you to develop a clearer vision that keeps you on track.

Having a clear vision before setting goals for whatever you desire in life is of utmost importance, as it provides the golden thread that connects your dreams and acts as the guiding light at the end of the tunnel. When it comes to achieving balance, setting clear, meaningful, and attainable, although stretching, goals are essential.

By establishing a compelling vision, you lay the foundation for setting aspirational goals that are both challenging and achievable. A vision serves as the driving force behind your goals, aligning them with your overall purpose and direction. It provides you with a sense of clarity and purpose, allowing you to prioritise your resources, time, energy, and well-being effectively.

When you have a clear vision in place, you can manage your resources more efficiently. It enables you to make conscious decisions about how to allocate your time and energy in a way that supports your goals and aligns with your values. By avoiding overextending, yourself or spreading your resources too thin, you can prevent burnout and maintain a sustainable pace towards your desired outcomes.

Moreover, a vision acts as a constant reminder of what truly matters to you. It keeps you focused and motivated, even when faced with challenges or distractions along the way. When your goals are rooted in a compelling vision, you can stay resilient and persevere through obstacles, knowing that the light at the end of the tunnel is worth the effort.

By integrating vision into your goal-setting process, you create a harmonious synergy between your aspirations and your actions. Goals become more than just mere tasks; they become steppingstones towards your desired future. The vision acts as the golden thread that ties everything together, ensuring that each goal contributes to the bigger picture and leads you closer to your designed *Wealth Beyond Money*.

Remember: Having a clear vision prior to goal setting is essential to achieving balance and success.

Set Aspirational Goals

The main thing to know is that you are goal-driven all of the time, and everything you do is to achieve something you want.

Setting goals that link to your strategic plan is paramount to achieving your desired outcome.

Make your unconscious goals conscious and make your goals yours rather than those of someone else. You are influenced by all that has gone before, and many of your goals and habits will have been inherited from others.

There is a book on this specific subject on Amazon and Audible called *Goal Setting for Change*, written by Julie Hogbin.

Implement Boundaries

Boundaries are a crucial component of life mastery, which is exactly what creating *Wealth Beyond Money* entails. Boundaries enable compassion, creating a sense of order and understanding in your interactions with others and with yourself. Establishing clear and healthy boundaries helps you effectively manage your time, energy, and emotions, which are fundamental aspects of life mastery. It empowers you to prioritise your needs and goals, thereby fostering self-respect and personal growth.

Establishing your boundaries creates a standard that you deliver for yourself and accept from others. Boundaries form a line where you set your giving and receiving acceptance; boundaries are you defining what is okay and what is not okay for you personally.

Setting boundaries is a means of self-care and being more compassionate to others. A boundary is a *thing* that, once crossed, becomes something else! It is important to set healthy boundaries for all you do in life, for when the line is crossed, all *sorts* of things can happen. Some boundaries you cross knowingly for yourself, and yours may be crossed unknowingly by others, just as you may cross others unknowingly.

Counterintuitively, setting boundaries promotes compassion by encouraging empathy and respect for others' space and feelings. Without boundaries, it is easy to inadvertently infringe on others' rights or overlook your own needs, leading to imbalance and conflict. The mastery of boundaries and their communication is pivotal for personal development and compassionate interaction with the world around us.

Set Healthy Boundaries

Boundaries are applicable across every aspect of every relationship you participate in through life, both business and personal. It is important to recognise that each person's boundaries will be different from yours and will reflect their unique needs, values, and comfort levels. Ultimately, boundaries serve as vital guidelines that shape healthy interactions and ensure mutual respect, and they are often established to maintain a productive and respectful environment.

When individuals understand that there are repercussions for crossing boundaries, they are more likely to respect the personal and professional space of others. Boundaries are effective when consequences exist for their abuse, and the consequences are implemented and carried through:

- **Communicate physical and emotional needs**: Setting strict boundaries will help you tell others what you want and need on a physical and emotional level and enable you to express the discomfort you may experience.
- **Power balance**: Power dynamics play a significant role and are essential to recognise, define, and maintain to establish healthy boundaries. It is fundamental to recognise and understand these dynamics to ensure respect, balance, and reciprocity. These power differences may be rooted in social, economic, or personal factors, and when acknowledged, they pave the way for balanced interactions. Conscious recognition and negotiation of the power dynamic contribute to healthier, more respectful relationships where both parties feel valued and heard.

- **Privacy and confidentiality**: Knowing what information will be shared is an integral element in boundary setting, particularly in relationships that involve the sharing of personal or sensitive information. Knowing that respect and protection of personal information are on the agenda, create a safe and trusted space where each individual feels comfortable sharing their thoughts, feelings, dreams, and experiences.
- **Vulnerability** plays a critical role in setting boundaries and enhancing communication within relationships. Being open about your needs, emotions, and limitations requires a level of courage and vulnerability in your *Leadership Voice* that deepens trust and understanding. It encourages transparent communication, allowing both parties to express their feelings without fear of judgment and developing a culture of mutual respect and compassion. Remember, that once information is shared, it cannot be retrieved.
- **Cultivate Mutual Respect**: Expressing your boundaries to others signifies your self-respect, and when others honour your boundaries, it reflects their respect towards you. It is a constructive exchange that fosters a culture of mutual respect and understanding.

- **Assert Your Needs**: Establishing boundaries empowers you to confidently articulate your desires and convictions. It is a bold expression of self-advocacy, demonstrating your readiness to uphold your needs and beliefs.

Creating new blueprints for you and the relationships in your life and combining them with your improved blueprints for your health and financial status will provide you with the increased wellness that brings you closer to creating true *Wealth Beyond Money*, the multi-dimensional vision for you all.

Manage Your Time Effectively

In reality, you cannot manage time; however, you can manage your activities to maximise the time available more effectively, which is crucial for achieving balance. Prioritise your tasks and activities, and make sure that you allocate time that gives you enough time for the things that matter most.

This will help you stay focused, organised, and productive.

> *Remember*: You all have the same amount of time to do with as you will, and some use it more wisely than others. How do you use the time available to you?

Develop a Growth Mindset

Developing a growth mindset and flow is crucial for your personal and professional development. It refers to the belief that your abilities and intelligence can be developed through dedication, effort, and perseverance — it means you believe in yourself.

Having a growth mindset is essential because it promotes resilience, adaptability, and continuous learning. It encourages you to embrace challenges as opportunities for growth and view setbacks as temporary obstacles that can be overcome through effort and learning.

With a growth mindset, you are more likely to put in the necessary effort, seek out new knowledge, and persist in the face of difficulties. This mindset fosters a positive attitude, drives personal and professional success, and enables you to maximise your potential. A growth mindset allows you to approach life with a positive attitude and to be open to new experiences and ideas. This will help you overcome obstacles and achieve your goals.

> *Remember*: A great mind-flow and self-belief will power you through.

CHAPTER 7:
The Ideal Way to Balance Your Life

Balance is a masterpiece we create for our life.

–Julie Hogbin

Keeping the old-fashioned scales in mind, consider using the following six segments of life as the weights you place on the scale to find balance:

- Your relationships, both personal and business
- Your personal and spiritual growth
- Your health: physical, mental, and emotional
- Your friends and family
- Your career or business interests
- Your finances

Each of these segments requires attention so that you can create true wealth. If you spend too much time on only one segment, you will end up neglecting the others. However, if you shift the time and energy you spend on each segment, you will distribute the weight on your scale more equally, resulting in a more balanced life.

An example of an unbalanced life is how having money in the bank doesn't necessarily result in wealth. If you are overly focused on your career or other business interests, your bank account may look promising. However, you may well neglect the other two philosophies of wealth: your health and your relationships. You may be spending so much time at work that you are neglecting your family and friends. This can cause difficulty in your relationships with others and result in feelings of isolation, loneliness, and a sense of disconnection, which can lead to serious mental health issues such as anxiety disorder and depression. If you do not have meaningful relationships, it doesn't matter how successful you become or how much money you may have in the bank; you will have no one to share it with or grow old with.

Moreover, when you prioritise your career to the extreme, it can have adverse effects on your physical well-being. It may lead to chronic fatigue, disrupt your sleep patterns, and weaken your immune system, making it difficult for you to fully enjoy your daily life. The constant stress and pressure from work can also heighten feelings of anxiety and irritability, straining your relationships with others even further. Additionally, poor health can lead to increased health or medical expenses, resulting in less money available for other purposes. It is essential to prioritise your health to ensure you have the vitality to thrive in all areas of your life.

If you work on creating a good balance between your career, health, and relationships, you will create more happiness, overall fulfilment, and, therefore, true wealth in your life. When it comes to relationships, it's important to keep in mind that the most important one you should work on is your relationship with yourself. To do this, there are various self-care practices you can include in your daily life, such as regular exercise, proper nutrition, engaging in activities that bring you joy, and making sure you get proper rest.

Having a strong and positive relationship with oneself is of utmost importance, as it lays the foundation for all other relationships in life. When you have a healthy and loving relationship with yourself, you are better equipped to handle the challenges and stresses that come with work, finances, and other life demands. You can maintain a clear and balanced perspective and make decisions that are aligned with your values and well-being. Moreover, a strong sense of self-awareness and self-love enables you to approach your relationships with others positively and healthily, create more meaningful connections, and be truer in your interactions with others.

When you consider creating more balance in your life, it's important to keep in mind that having a balanced life and creating *Wealth Beyond Money* will look different to all people. As a result, there's no universal approach to creating balance. This will depend on your personal circumstances and needs. Look at the six segments listed above and prioritise each area of your life, both according to your current needs and future desires. Rate each of these segments on a scale from one to ten, with ten being excellent and one requiring a lot of improvement. Your rating of the six segments will help you identify which areas of your life require more attention as well as where you may spend way too much of your time and energy.

Next, make a list of all the areas you need to prioritise to create true wealth in your life. You may find that there are specific areas in your life that need more attention, such as your personal or spiritual growth, your relationships, or improving your physical or mental health. This self-reflection will help you identify the areas that need more attention and investment to create a life that is more balanced. The closer you are to rating these aspects similarly, the closer you are to creating true wealth and fulfilment in your life.

Once you have made your list of priorities, pick the areas of your life that you need to pay more attention to. Set clear and stretching goals, in your identified areas and create a plan to help you reach them. The path to a balanced life, with focus and determination, you will achieve anything you truly want enough.

Even if there are more areas you want to work on, resist the urge to take them all on simultaneously. Doing this will result in you attempting to make too many changes at the same time and, as a result, increase your risk of getting overwhelmed. Instead, focus on the most important areas, and once you are comfortable with these changes and have reached your goals, relook at your priority list, and create new goals for yourself.

Remember: You are working towards balance and flow across all areas.

Secrets to a Balanced Life

*Doubt can motivate you, so don't be afraid of it.
Confidence and doubt are at two ends of the scale,
and you need both. They balance each other out.*

–**Barbra Streisand**

Living a balanced life means making sure the different and smaller aspects of your life fit together to create a bigger picture. Think of your life as a giant puzzle. Various pieces of this puzzle must fit together perfectly to create the full picture. If a single piece doesn't fit into the puzzle or goes missing, it is immediately noticeable.

Now, think of creating *Wealth Beyond Money* like building a puzzle. Every aspect of your life needs to fit together to create the happiness and fulfilment needed to create the true wealth you desire. This is why it's important to take stock of your life so that you can determine which pieces of the puzzle you may need to work on to create the perfect picture.

Creating a balanced life is a gradual process that demands intentional action. To step out of your comfort zone and thrive, develop healthy habits that enhance your well-being. These habits will propel you towards your aspirations of genuine prosperity.

Prioritise Self-Care

Taking care of yourself is not selfish; it is essential to living a balanced life. You need to make time for activities that help you relax and rejuvenate, whether it's taking a massage, reading, meditating, or enjoying a hobby. When you take care of yourself, you will also work to improve your physical, emotional, and mental health. This will help you improve your focus on the aspects you have prioritised to create true wealth. When you are on an aeroplane, and the safety instructions are given? The instruction is, "When the oxygen mask drops, you put yours on first before helping others." If you do not take care of yourself first, then you will not be able to help anyone else. It is exactly the same in life. Taking care of yourself is like putting on an oxygen mask. It is not being selfish; it is vital.

Cultivate Healthy Relationships

Strong and supportive relationships are essential for a balanced life. Surround yourself with people who encourage, motivate, and inspire you and who help you grow and achieve your goals. Nurture these relationships by being honest, present, supportive, and a great communicator. Work on becoming an active listener during conversations rather than responding immediately. Being a great listener is aided by making sure your body language stays open while the other person talks, nodding in agreement, and confirming that you understood the other person by paraphrasing their words before you respond, for example, "So, if I heard and understood you correctly, what you're saying is..."

> *Remember*: Your network is your net worth in far more ways than money.

Pursue Hobbies and Interests

Discovering what you are passionate about and finding purpose in your life will help you achieve a sense of fulfilment and balance. When you are engaged in activities that you are passionate about, you will feel more energised, focused, and motivated. These can be hobbies to help you relax or more things that really interest you during your scheduled time for self-care.

Now, some hobbies may serve more than one purpose, such as linking fitness to inclusion and building relationships through groups—or reading for spiritual growth and a book club to discuss the subject matter.

Remember: Nothing sits in isolation; everything is connected. Look for connections and join the dots in everything you do.

Practise Gratitude

Gratitude and mindfulness will help you stay present and appreciate the good things in your life. Take time to reflect on the positive aspects of your life and cultivate a sense of gratitude for them. Make a habit of naming something out loud that you're grateful for at specific times every day, for example, when you sit down for dinner. Your brain reacts differently to things that you hear as opposed to things that you think. Therefore, saying it out loud will be more effective in helping you feel more grateful for what you have in your life.

Practising gratitude helps shift your focus from what you lack to what you have, fostering a positive mindset and promoting overall well-being. It cultivates a sense of contentment and satisfaction with the present moment, reducing feelings of stress, anxiety, and dissatisfaction.

Being grateful helps you gain perspective and find meaning in challenging situations. It reminds you of the positive aspects of life, even in difficult times, allowing you to approach obstacles with resilience and hope.

On a practical level, gratitude is the number one thing to do. If you are not grateful for what you have, why would anyone or anything give you more?

Deep Breathing and Meditation

Deep breathing and meditation are powerful tools for reducing stress and promoting a sense of calm. When you are stressed, your body responds by breathing faster, which can actually exacerbate feelings of anxiety and panic. By practising deep breathing, you take control of your breathing rate and slow your heart rate, which will help you feel calmer and more in control. By focusing on your breath, you will quiet your mind and relax your body, which can be especially helpful during times of stress or anxiety.

Incorporating regular deep breathing and meditation practices into your routine will help you become more self-aware and centred. When you meditate, you are essentially taking time to focus on yourself and remove distractions, which will be incredibly empowering. Through regular practice, you will learn to tune out external distractions and focus on your internal thoughts and feelings, which will help you better understand yourself and your own needs. Whether you are looking to reduce stress, increase focus, or simply take some time to unwind, deep breathing and meditation will be incredibly valuable tools in your self-care toolkit.

Exercise

Exercise not only improves physical health; it also has a significant impact on your mental and emotional well-being. When you engage in physical activity, your brain releases a chemical called dopamine, which is responsible for feelings of happiness and pleasure. This chemical helps to alleviate stress and anxiety, boosts mood, and increases energy levels. Exercise also helps to release tension and clear your mind, promoting mental clarity and focus. Additionally, the discipline required to maintain an exercise routine helps to cultivate mental strength and resilience. Even though exercise may not be your favourite activity, the huge benefits are undeniable, as are the positive effects on your overall health.

Find a type of exercise that you will enjoy, and that fits around your lifestyle, whether it's dancing, hiking, running, swimming, going to the gym, or playing a sport. By making exercise a priority and incorporating it into your daily routine, you will not only maintain a healthy body, but you will also improve your mental and emotional well-being. Regardless of whether you have a full hour to spare or just a few minutes, any effort you make towards physical activity is a step towards a healthier and happier you.

Discipline is something you will need when you are creating wealth for yourself. You will need to be mentally sound to deal with tough situations and make the right choices. Exercising regularly helps you build this mental strength. This is evident by the number of successful CEOs and businesspeople who choose to make exercise a priority in their lives.

Richard Branson, who has multiple business ventures, famously said, "I seriously doubt that I would have been as successful in my career (and happy in my personal life) if I hadn't always placed importance on my health and fitness." The Shark Tank businessman, Mark Cuban, shares the same sentiment: "That I will find a way to get (a workout) done, I think, reflects how relentless I can be in the business world as well" (Ginsberg, 2017). If these successful people and many others place such a huge importance on working out, then there is a lesson for us all to learn from and implement in our lives.

Build Positive Associations

Conditioning yourself for success through building positive associations involves consciously reinforcing positive beliefs, thoughts, and behaviours to create new neural pathways in your brain. This process is based on neuroplasticity, the brain's ability to adapt and change in response to new experiences and learning. Which ultimately embeds the new blueprint into your unconscious and creates a new or refined habit, enabling you to operate automatically, making things easier. By consciously focusing on positive associations, you can rewire your brain to increase positive outcomes in your life.

Let's look at an example. When you have always enjoyed food from a specific chain of restaurant, you automatically associate the logo for this restaurant with enjoyable food. When you see this logo, you will feel hungry, regardless of whether you just had a meal or not. Another example may be putting on certain music or binaural beats when you want to concentrate. If you have worked on conditioning your mind to focus when you hear these sounds or music, you will be able to focus a lot easier.

Let's look at an example of an association linked to health with regular exercise. By consistently engaging in physical activity, you create associations with exercise, such as increased energy, improved mood, and better physical health. Over time, your brain associates exercise with these positive feelings, making maintaining an exercise routine easier and more enjoyable. This positive association also leads to other positive behaviours, such as healthier food choices, quality of sleep, and reduced stress levels. Ultimately, your positive association with exercise improves your overall health and creates a loop that reinforces healthy habits.

An example of a negative association linked to money is feeling anxious or stressed about financial insecurity or debt. This negative association can lead to various negative behaviours and emotions related to money, such as overspending, compulsive shopping, or avoiding financial responsibility altogether. For example, someone who has struggled with debt in the past may feel overwhelmed and anxious about their financial situation, which can lead them to avoid checking their bank account or bills or even to make impulsive purchases to alleviate their stress temporarily. This negative association with money can create a cycle of financial instability and stress, ultimately impacting overall financial health and well-being. Overcoming negative emotional associations that result in a poor relationship with money requires a conscious effort to address underlying beliefs and behaviours related to money, such as seeking financial guidance, developing healthy spending habits, and practicing positive self-talk and visualisation to create a more positive association with money.

Design your new positive associations consciously, and then plan how to create the positive associations, creating the new habits you need to achieve your goals. Create the impact you desire in all areas. The process works with all aspects of *Wealth Beyond Money*, including relationships and life or business issues.

The unconscious mind plays a significant role in building these positive associations, as it processes and stores information that is not consciously accessible to you. By reinforcing positive thoughts and behaviours over time, you create new neural pathways in the brain that become automatic and unconscious, leading to more positive outcomes in your life without you even realising it. You create new habits.

Building positive associations linked to personal blueprints and the unconscious involves a conscious effort to focus on your primary values, positive beliefs, thoughts, and experiences, reinforcing them over time to create new neural pathways in the brain that lead to positive outcomes in your life and *Wealth Beyond Money*.

Manage Your Finances

Since the money in your bank account is an important part of creating true wealth, it's crucial that you work on managing your finances more effectively. This will include investing your money wisely by ensuring that you have a diversified portfolio of investments that includes financial instruments such as stocks, bonds, and other asset classes to grow your wealth over time. You may think that currently, you do not have the resources for a varied portfolio; however, we are in the age of innovation and technology, and there are now many platforms or online apps, that allow you to invest from as little as £1 or $1. There are no excuses not to start working on your finances. Begin small by using whatever money you can save to invest.

There is a saying, "You do not have to be great to get started; however, you have to get started to be great."

Establish a budget that reflects your income and expenses and track your spending to ensure you are staying within your means. No matter how much you might want to purchase a new possession or go on a trip, make sure you can afford it before you splurge unnecessarily. Set aside money each month for emergency savings and long-term goals, such as retirement or a down payment on a home.

If you have debt, create a plan to pay it off as soon as possible. Prioritise your high-interest debt and consider consolidating or refinancing it if it will help you pay off your debt sooner. If you choose to consolidate your debt, do not build it up again through misspending.

Remember: Building a balanced life is an ongoing process that requires practice and self-awareness. It cannot be achieved overnight, however with consistent effort and dedication, it is possible to find balance.

Types of Leverage

Knowledge Leverage

Knowledge is a valuable asset that can be leveraged to gain an advantage in various aspects of life. It involves acquiring and utilising information to make informed decisions and take calculated actions. By investing time and effort in learning and acquiring new skills, you can leverage that knowledge to excel in your personal and professional lives. Continuous learning, attending courses or workshops, or acquiring additional qualifications (if required) can provide you with a competitive edge.

For example, if you're starting a new business, you can leverage your knowledge by researching the market, understanding customer needs, and staying updated on industry trends. This will enable you to make smart choices and stay ahead of the competition.

People Leverage

Building and nurturing relationships with the right people can be a game-changer. Leveraging involves tapping into the expertise, experiences, and networks of others to achieve your goals. For instance, if you're looking to expand your professional network, you can leverage the connections of your mentors, colleagues, or industry influencers. By seeking guidance and collaborating with people who have already achieved success in your desired field, you can accelerate your progress and open doors to new opportunities. Networking events, professional associations, and online platforms are great avenues to expand your network.

> *Remember*: every network is different, and not every network knows every network; they operate in their own "bubbles."

Time Leverage

Time is a precious resource and leveraging it effectively can significantly impact your productivity and success. Time leverage involves optimising your time by prioritising tasks, eliminating time-wasting activities, delegating responsibilities, and automating processes. Plus, using time management techniques or time-blocking can help you make the most of your time and accomplish more in a focused manner.

For instance, if you're running a business, you can leverage your time by outsourcing non-core activities or utilising technology to streamline repetitive tasks. By doing so, you free up time to focus on high-value activities that drive growth and create more opportunities.

Technology and Tools Leverage

Utilising technology and tools can significantly increase your capabilities. Whether it is using productivity apps, software, automation tools, or leveraging online platforms and resources, technology can streamline processes, increase efficiency, and enable you to accomplish more in less time.

Personal Leverage

This is when you leverage your connections and relationships with others to help you move forward in life. Your network is directly linked to your net worth. It is so important to have a great network in many different networks, including business and social networks. Research indicates that you are the sum of the five people you spend the majority of your time with. Have a look around and assess the trueness of this statement for yourself and your network.

Remember: Your personal leverage is a reciprocity-based activity; you give and take.

Mentoring and Coaching Leverage

Leveraging the expertise and guidance of mentors or coaches can accelerate your personal and professional development. They provide insights, guidance, and support based on their experiences, helping you avoid mistakes, gain new perspectives, and achieve your goals faster.

Mentoring and *Coaching* can be paid or unpaid, formal, or informal. Regardless of which combination you access, ensure you know what you are agreeing to and that it will be of benefit to you. You can always make more money, but you can never recoup the time and energy expended.

Finance Leverage

Financial leverage involves utilising borrowed funds or other financial instruments to increase your potential returns. For example, if you're interested in investing in real estate, you can leverage your funds by taking out a mortgage or partnering with other investors. This allows you to access larger opportunities and potentially amplify your returns. Example: The investment or assets generate a higher amount than the loan. Simple example: Borrow £20,000 for a small shop or lock up and rent the premises. The monthly rental payment is £500, less the loan payment of £300. Monthly Profit: £200. This is where leveraged debt is utilised for you to benefit from your investments.

To best use leverage in your day-to-day life, it is essential to have a clear understanding of your goals and align your efforts accordingly. Identify the areas where leverage can make the most significant impact and develop a plan to leverage your resources effectively.

By applying knowledge leverage, surrounding yourself with the right people, and strategically using other forms of leverage, you can create a powerful synergy that propels you towards your goals. Embrace the concept of leverage, seize opportunities, and watch as you unlock new levels of success in your journey towards *Wealth Beyond Money.*

Leverage is about using resources, knowledge, relationships, and tools strategically to multiply your efforts and achieve better results. However, it's essential to assess risks, make informed decisions, and maintain a balance to ensure that the leverage you employ aligns with your goals and values.

> ***Remember***: Leverage is smartly utilising the resources available to you.

CHAPTER 9:
Create Your New Blueprints

Determine Your Health Blueprint

When it comes to your health, it's important to have a plan in place. This is where determining your personal health blueprint comes in. By assessing your current health status, identifying areas for improvement, and setting goals for achieving optimal physical, mental, and emotional well-being, you can take charge of your health and improve the quality of your life.

To get started, here are some steps you can follow to identify your personal health blueprint:

> *Remember*: You all have mental health; it cannot be seen, and it requires love and attention.

- **Assess your current health status**: To create a blueprint for optimal physical, mental, and emotional well-being, you need to start by assessing your current health status. Take a moment to consider your physical health, mental health, and emotional well-being. Try to identify any health concerns or conditions that may require attention.

- **Identify areas for improvement**: To determine your health blueprint, it's essential to identify areas for improvement. Take a moment to consider what you'd like to improve about your health. Do you want to eat healthier, exercise more, reduce stress, improve your sleep quality, or address mental health concerns? By identifying areas that need improvement, you can create a plan to achieve your health goals.

- **Identify your reasons**: When it comes to making changes in your life, it's important to understand the underlying reasons for your behaviour. Many of your actions are driven by psychological factors that you may not even be aware of. To create lasting change, it's essential to identify these factors and question them. For example, if you have a habit of procrastinating, it may be because you are afraid of failure or success or because you are seeking short-term pleasure over long-term benefits. By questioning these underlying beliefs, you can begin to reframe your thinking and change your behaviour. Similarly, if you struggle with overeating, it may be because of emotional eating or a lack of awareness of hunger cues. By examining the reasons behind your eating habits, you can begin to address them and make healthier choices.

- **Set specific goals**: Set clear and specific goals that are achievable and relevant to your personal health blueprint. For instance, if you want to improve your eating habits, set a goal of consuming a specific set of good calories every day and avoid foods you know you should. This is very simple and easy to do with apps such as MyFitnessPal.

Remember: Not every calorie is equal.

- **Create an action plan**: If you want to increase your physical activity, set yourself a goal to exercise for at least 30 minutes at least three times a week. Make sure your goals are realistic and measurable and have a timeline to track your progress and celebrate your achievements.

- **Get support**: Surrounding yourself with supportive people can be a great motivator when it comes to achieving your health goals. Consider seeking support from a healthcare provider, therapist, or coach if you have extra funds in your budget. These professionals provide guidance and accountability, and help you overcome any obstacles you may face. Additionally, surround yourself with friends and family who are supportive and encourage healthy choices. Having a strong support system can make a big difference in your success.

- **Stay committed**: Stay dedicated to your health blueprint and remain patient as you work towards achieving your health and fitness goals. Recognise and celebrate your successes along the way, and, if and when necessary, make adjustments to your plan. Building healthy habits takes time and effort; however, the benefits to your overall well-being are more than worth it. Stay motivated and committed to your health and wellness journey.

- **Get the basics right**: The first step in adopting a healthy lifestyle is to make sure you have the basics. This will be highly dependent on how you currently live and the changes you may have to make in your life. Some of these basics can include:

    o Reduce your salt intake by using herbs and spices to flavour your meals instead of salt. Too much salt can lead to high blood pressure and other health problems.

    o Limit your consumption of sugary foods and drinks, such as candy, soda, and desserts. Instead, choose healthier options like fresh fruits or unsweetened snacks. Overeating can lead to weight gain and other health issues.

    o Avoid overeating by practicing mindful eating techniques, such as eating slowly and stopping when you feel full.

    o Make healthy food choices by including a variety of fruits, vegetables, whole grains, lean proteins, and healthy fats in your diet. This can help you maintain a healthy weight and reduce your risk of chronic diseases.

- Drink alcohol in moderation, which means less than one drink per day for women and up to two drinks for men. Drinking too much alcohol can lead to liver disease, high blood pressure, and other health problems.

- Incorporate daily exercise into your routine, such as taking a brisk walk, jogging, or doing yoga. Regular exercise will help you maintain a healthy weight, reduce stress, and improve your overall health.

- Stay hydrated by drinking plenty of water— between 1 and 3 litres throughout the day. The health benefits are immense, from weight loss to flushing your kidneys. Dehydration often leads to fatigue, headaches, and other health problems.

- Quit smoking, as it can increase your risk of lung cancer, heart disease, and other serious health issues. Seek support from a healthcare provider or smoking cessation programme if you need help quitting.

Your personal health blueprint is unique to you, and it may change as your health status evolves over time. Therefore, it is important to assess your health regularly and adjust your goals and actions accordingly to achieve optimal physical, mental, and emotional well-being. Keep in mind that progress may take time; be patient and stay committed to your health goals. By following these steps, you will create a blueprint for a much healthier and happier you.

Determine Your Emotional Health Blueprint

Understanding your emotional blueprint, is of utmost importance, as it allows you to navigate the intricate landscape of your own emotions and inner world, which, of course, impacts your outer world.

There is a phrase commonly used that is "you made me feel," and this is an opportunity for you to take ownership; if you have not already, that no one can make you feel anything—it is your choice to feel. Personal responsibility is key in this area, and of course, who you are is a product of all that has gone before in your life.

Learn how to express your emotions in a healthy manner. It is important to acknowledge and process both positive and negative emotions. You have them and suppressing them is not healthy. Learning how to express them effectively is vital for your balance in all relationships.

By recognising and determining the root cause of your emotional patterns, triggers, and tendencies, you gain insight into the reason for your feelings and reactions. Reflect on your repeated experiences of emotions—are they supporting you or hindering you?

> *Remember*: Understanding what causes your emotions and how they affect you and your results, allows you to become more self-aware, which then allows for reflection and growth.

Identify Your Relationship Blueprint

As a wise person once said, "people come into your life for a *Reason*, a *Season*, or a *Lifetime*"; which relationship are you looking for?

> *Remember*: The one relationship you will have for life is the one with yourself.

Having strong relationships in your life will contribute to your creating the *Wealth Beyond Money* that you desire. This will help you build strong bonds with others that you need as a support system in your life. Your relationship blueprint focus will cover romantic relationships, your career and business relationships, your friendships, and most importantly, the relationship you have with yourself.

Your relationship with yourself, can be regarded as your most important one. If you are happy with yourself as a person, know who you are, and know what you want in life, you will be able to bring this confidence into your relationships and make sure the people in your life are aware of what you want and what your personal limits are, for what you are willing to give and receive.

Take some time to think about how you feel about yourself and whether you are happy with where you are in your life, your career, your relationships, and your health. Are you spending enough time doing things that you enjoy and that help you relax? Are you making enough time for yourself? If you feel like your self-care is lacking, it is important that you first make more of an effort in this aspect of your life, before you work on your other relationships.

Remember: Your relationship with yourself will positively and negatively impact any other relationship in your life; you must get your most intimate relationship healthy.

Self-Relationship

This above all: to thine own self be true, and it must follow, as the night the day, thou canst not then be false to any man.

–William Shakespeare

Loving and respecting yourself are the foundation for your overall mental, emotional, and physical health. Remember that the journey to self-love and respect is personal and unique for everyone, and it may take time. There is no set timeline; be patient with yourself. It is okay to take small steps, to ask for help if you need it, and to start if you haven't already.

Remember, how you feel and think about yourself affects every external relationship you enter into, for good or bad. The emotions and memories you carry with you from an early age and every relationship you have been in throughout your life, affect you now and can all be destructured, leaving you free and clean for what comes next in your future.

> **Remember:** perfection is in the eye of the beholder and does not exist in reality—what is perfect? We are all a work in progress.

Your relationship blueprint with yourself will be made up of every interaction you have had throughout your life, starting from what you heard and experienced when you were in the womb through your upbringing, education, and life so far.

It will be how you speak to yourself, how you allow others to speak to you, what boundaries you have in place, and how you treat yourself—there is a long list to consider, and please refer back to Chapter 2.

Here are some key principles to work your way through:

1. **Understanding Self-Worth**: This is the realisation that you are valuable and worthwhile just as you are. You do not need to earn your value or worth by fulfilling other people's expectations. You are deserving of respect, kindness, and love because of who you are as a human being, not what you do or achieve.

2. **Self-Care**: Loving yourself means taking care of your physical, emotional, and mental health. This can include exercising, eating healthy, getting enough sleep, engaging in relaxing activities, and seeking help when you need it, whether from trusted friends, family, or mental health professionals. Self-care is not selfish; it is vital. You cannot drink from an empty well, give from an empty purse, or feed from an empty larder.

3. **Setting Boundaries**: This is a key aspect of self-respect. By setting boundaries, you protect your time, energy, and emotional health. This can involve saying "No" when you need to, deciding who gets to be part of your life, and defining what behaviours you will or will not accept from others.

4. **Mindfulness and Self-Compassion**: Mindfulness helps you stay present and avoid self-judgement. Self-compassion encourages you to treat yourself with the same kindness and understanding you would extend to others. Both of these practices can help you handle difficult feelings and circumstances, reducing stress and promoting emotional well-being.

5. **Personal Growth**: Continual learning and self-improvement can build self-respect and self-love. This can involve developing new skills, expanding your knowledge, or addressing personal weaknesses. However, it is important to balance this with self-acceptance, understanding that it's okay not to be perfect.

6. **Gratitude and recognition**: Regularly acknowledging what you appreciate about yourself, your life, and what you are good at will improve your self-esteem, confidence, and general outlook.

7. **Forgiveness**: Letting go of past mistakes is crucial for self-love. Everyone makes mistakes; it's part of being human. By forgiving yourself, you can let go of guilt and regret, allowing you to move forward.

8. **Positive Self-Talk**: How you talk to yourself matters. Replace critical or negative thoughts with positive, affirming ones. Control that inner voice, which sometimes talks out loud as well. This will improve your self-perception and general mood.

9. **Find Your Passion and Purpose**: Doing what you love and what drives you will help you feel happier and more fulfilled, contributing to self-love and respect.

10. **Embrace Your Individuality**: You are unique, with your own strengths, weaknesses, and quirks. Embrace this individuality. Celebrate your strengths and acknowledge your weaknesses without judgment.

If you put the above 10 points on a scale and assessed yourself against them, how would you score your blueprint relationship with yourself?

Remember: You are your own gold and diamond and platinum.

Romantic Relationship

The meeting of two personalities is like the contact of two chemical substances: if there is any reaction, both are transformed.

—Carl Gustav Jung

Oh, the joy of being in love and the heartbreak of it ending—and why do they end? You either grow together or grow apart and when you grow apart, do you stay, or do you leave?

Imagine bringing all of you and all of someone else together with all your individual histories coming together—you can see how there is a potential tinder box created.

There are many models and theories we could have added to this book, and many are great and will help. There are many personality profiling tools that will assess both of your personalities and create a joint understanding that can be worked with. And, let's get real:

What attracted you to each other in the first place? What happened to that attraction?

When you meet and fall in love, there is a chemical reaction and attraction; it is like two opposite poles coming together, and fittingly, not only is there love, but there will also be lust. It is a vital part of intimate relationships. Now, depending on your age and even in the latter years, physical attraction counts, and of course, what is attractiveness? It will be different for each of you.

Lust tends to focus more on the physical aspect of attraction and less on emotional connection or long-term compatibility. Lust is powerful and can overlook the finer points of relationships.

In the context of relationships, lust is often one of the first stages, where individuals feel a strong pull towards each other based largely on physical attraction. However, for a relationship to be healthy and sustainable in the long term, it generally needs more than just lust; it also requires emotional intimacy, mutual respect, shared values, and other components of love.

Love is a complex and multifaceted emotion that is universally experienced and cherished across cultures and genders. While there may not be one definitive definition of love that is universally agreed upon, there are common themes and understandings.

Love can be described as a deep affection, attachment, and connection that exists between individuals. It is often characterised by feelings of warmth, care, empathy, and a genuine desire for the well-being and happiness of the loved one. Love encompasses both emotional and behavioural aspects, involving a range of emotions such as joy, happiness, tenderness, and compassion.

In the context of romantic relationships, love takes on a unique significance. It involves a deep emotional and physical attraction, accompanied by a strong desire for intimacy, companionship, and mutual understanding. It often includes elements of passion, romance, and sexual attraction. It is a powerful force that can inspire individuals to make sacrifices, commit to each other, and navigate the challenges that come with a long-term partnership.

What love means to each person is deeply personal and subjective. It can be influenced by one's cultural background, personal experiences, values, and beliefs. Love is a journey of self-discovery, growth, and vulnerability. It involves accepting and embracing both the joys and challenges that come with caring deeply for another person.

Your romantic relationship blueprint will be founded on your current set of beliefs, expectations, and behaviours around relationships that you have developed over time. It is shaped by a variety of influences and experiences. This is how it will typically form, and remember that this will be different for you and your partner.

Early family and caregiver dynamics are the first and perhaps most influential relationships you observe and partake in. Your early caregivers can be immediate, combined family, institutional, or a combination of all. The way your parents, blended family, or caregivers interact with each other and with you creates the initial blueprint for what you view as "normal" in relationships. This includes how they communicate, express love, manage conflict, and respect boundaries.

Your past relationships, and with each relationship, your blueprint, continue to evolve. You learn from your experiences—both positive and negative—and each relationship can teach you something new, when you are open to it, about what you want, need, and expect from a partner, as well as what you offer in return.

We cannot leave out societal influences. Society and culture play a significant role in shaping your relationship blueprint. This includes societal norms and expectations, portrayals of relationships in the media, and cultural or religious beliefs about relationships.

Self-reflection and personal growth—intentionally or not—will significantly shape your relationship blueprint. The more you learn, the more you will be affected. Learning with and having shared or complementary interests with your partner supports cohesion.

This may involve reflecting on past relationships, considering what worked well and what didn't, identifying patterns, thinking about what you want for the future, and having that conversation. Personal growth can also involve learning new skills, such as communication or conflict resolution.

Remember that your relationship blueprint is not static; it can change and evolve over time as you gain new experiences, insights, and skills. It's okay—even healthy—to update your blueprint as you grow and change, especially if you are in a relationship that involves both of you.

Keeping a relationship exciting, sound, and long-lasting involves several key factors that require energy, effort, time, love, and patience:

> *You do not need Wi-Fi to have a conversation.* –Sharon Woolf

1. **Do what you did when you first met throughout your relationship, pure and simple**: You met and were attracted to each other for a reason; you got to know each other; you liked each other; you saw a future together; you pictured getting old or older together—keep doing what worked when you first met, in whichever way you can.

2. **Communication, Communication, Communication**: Open and honest communication is vital. This includes sharing your feelings, wants, needs, and concerns with each other, as well as listening to and understanding your partner's perspective. A relationship is not a one-way street.

3. **Mutual Respect**: Every person deserves to be treated with respect. This means acknowledging each other's individuality, feelings, desires, and opinions. It also means avoiding harmful behaviours such as insults, control, manipulation, and narcissistic behaviour.

4. **Trust**: Building trust takes time and consistency. Trust is not just about faithfulness in a romantic relationship; it's also about reliability, support, understanding, and having each other's back.

5. **Shared Experiences and Interests**: Doing things together helps keep the relationship fresh and exciting. This can involve shared hobbies, travel, or simply spending quality time together. At the same time, respect for individual interests and time apart is also important. Dependency is not considered healthy; therefore, personal interests and life are important and come together.

6. **Intimacy**: Emotional and physical intimacy are both important. This includes expressing love and affection, being vulnerable and open with each other, and maintaining a satisfying sexual relationship.

7. **Continued Growth**: You change over time; therefore, it is essential to grow together. This might involve setting shared goals, supporting each other's individual growth, and working through challenges together. It also includes one supporting the other and acknowledging that. What it doesn't mean is that both have to be high-flyer go-getters; what it does mean is that the support role is not taken for granted.

8. **Adaptability**: Life does throw you curveballs; flexibility and adaptability are key. This means adjusting to changes in circumstances, coping with stress or loss, and navigating transitions together.

9. **Maintaining a Sense of Appropriate Humour**: Laughter can ease stress, build connections, and make happy memories. Never underestimate the power of appropriate humour in a relationship.

10. **Regular Appreciation**: Express gratitude to each other regularly. Letting your partner know that you value them can deepen your bond and reinforce your relationship. Remember, how they want to be appreciated is not how you want to be appreciated—learn how to appreciate them for themselves in the way they do.

11. **Conflict Resolution Skills**: Every relationship has disagreements, and if you have no disagreements, something is not right. What is important is resolving or managing conflicts in a healthy way. Listening to each other, expressing your own feelings without blaming or criticising, and working together to find a solution. Remember, most conflict is caused by a goal being thwarted or hindered.

> *Remember*: each relationship is unique, and what works best can depend on various factors, including both partners' needs, personalities, and circumstances. If you have concerns about your relationship, seek support earlier rather than later.

There will be other relationships you have with friends, acquaintances, colleagues, and wider family members, and each will have its own blueprint depending on the beliefs and foundations you and they bring to the situation. Every relationship can be great or sour.

One of the main areas is to be honest and have open communication between all parties. Once the *secrets* start, and the resentments are not dealt with, any relationship can turn around and start to die. Sometimes, even with honest and transparent communication, relationships can falter and end, and that is okay. It is more beneficial to end an unhealthy relationship than live in torment and sadness.

There is a difference between being lonely and being alone, and being in a family group can be as lonely as living on your own, so we are told. Relationships are interesting areas of life that we can only control and manage ourselves, and of course, we cannot do that to another human. Well, let's say we should not do that to another human, and many try.

There is a recognition, that relationships transition through stages, and to make them work, all parties invest time, energy, and effort. It is a little like the relationship is in the third person; it is your personally created culture.

We will share one model that indicates how relationships grow and part, and it has a place for every relationship you will be in from life through career and business.

Knapp Relationship Model

Knapp's relational development model describes ten stages that relationships often go through. These stages were developed by communication researchers Mark L. Knapp and Anita L. Vangelisti. Here are the ten stages:

1. **Initiating**: This is the stage where you first meet and interact. You may exchange greetings, make introductions, and engage in small talk to establish initial contact.

2. **Experimenting**: In this stage, you start to gather more information about each other. You engage in casual conversations, ask questions, and explore common interests to determine if there is a potential for a deeper connection.

3. **Intensifying**: At this stage, you begin to develop a closer bond. You may start sharing personal information, revealing more about yourselves, and spending more time together. This stage often involves increased emotional and physical intimacy.

4. **Integrating**: In this stage, you become a couple or a recognised unit. You develop a shared identity, often referring to yourselves as "we" instead of "I" or "you." You may also engage in public displays of affection and become involved in each other's social circles. This also includes business as well.

5. **Bonding**: Bonding is the stage where the relationship becomes formalised, typically through a public declaration such as marriage, a commitment ceremony, or some other act that solidifies the relationship. It may be a business agreement.

6. **Differentiating**: In this stage, you start to regain your individual identities. You may begin to assert your personal interests and spend more time apart. Differences and conflicts may arise as you seek to maintain your autonomy.

7. **Circumscribing**: This stage involves a decrease in communication and a reduction of the relationship's breadth and depth. You may avoid certain topics or restrict interactions to superficial or mundane matters. This stage often signifies a decline in relationship satisfaction.

8. **Stagnation**: Stagnation occurs when a relationship becomes stale or stagnant. There is little growth or change, and communication may be minimal or repetitive. The relationship may feel stuck, and both individuals may feel dissatisfied or unfulfilled.

9. **Avoiding**: In this stage, you actively create distance and seek to minimise interaction with each other. You may avoid face-to-face encounters, find excuses to be unavailable, or intentionally engage in behaviours that keep you apart. This stage often indicates a significant deterioration in the relationship.

10. **Terminating**: The final stage is termination, where the relationship comes to an end. This can happen through various means, such as a breakup, divorce, or the death of one of the partners. Termination involves the formal or informal dissolution of the relationship, which can include you leaving a position, dismissal, or dissolution of a business.

It's important to note that not all relationships go through every stage; some will not progress further than stage one or two, and the duration of each stage can vary greatly depending on the individuals involved and the circumstances.

Knapp's Relationship Model

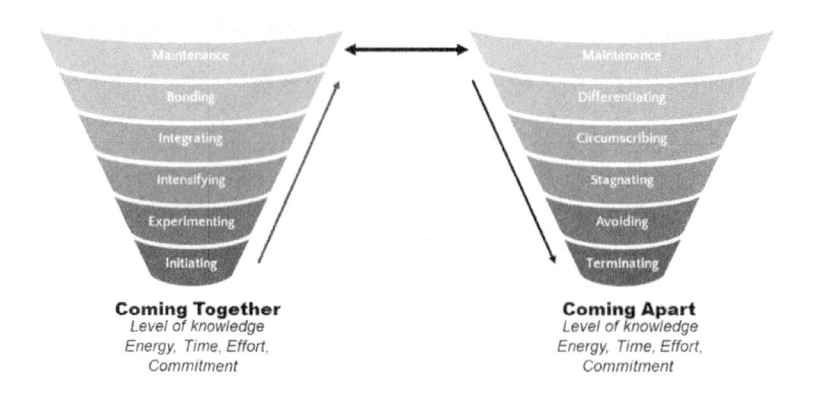

www.JulieHogbin.com

Coming Together
*Level of knowledge
Energy, Time, Effort,
Commitment*

- Maintenance
- Bonding
- Integrating
- Intensifying
- Experimenting
- Initiating

Coming Apart
*Level of knowledge
Energy, Time, Effort,
Commitment*

- Maintenance
- Differentiating
- Circumscribing
- Stagnating
- Avoiding
- Terminating

Also, accept that this process is followed with business partners and with your employer, if you have one. It is a process that can be adapted to all relationships. When you desire a relationship to work long-term, the main area to focus on, is the true foundational steps to getting to know one another, one through three—always ask those questions you need to ask. Check that your values are in alignment or are at least complimentary; check your beliefs; and if you both desire the same end result, do not assume.

Four and five are healthy areas, and if you find yourself slipping into six, do what you can to get back to five; six to nine is a slippery slope to travel, and 10, well, that is final, one way or the other.

Assess a couple of your current relationships against this model and see where you are and what you may need to do.

*The greatest enemy of knowledge is not ignorance,
it is the illusion of knowledge.*

–**Stephen Hawking**

Business Relationship Blueprint

Your business is only as strong as the relationships you build. Investing time and effort into building genuine connections can be the key to unlocking endless opportunities.

–**Sara Blakely**

I expect you will have heard the sayings "your network is your net worth" and "you are the average of the five people you spend most time with," and ultimately, this is the truth—it is, and you are.

What is the point of us mentioning this in a business blueprint chapter? *Because* you should be wary of who you get into business with, there is the saying "know, like, and trust," which pans out very well for business relationships.

If you are new to business, be cautious of new business partners and how far you get into business with them. Would you marry someone on the first date? No, then do not be in business with a stranger.

Spend the time, the energy, and the effort as you would for any relationship.

As with every personal relationship being different, every business relationship will be different because you are unique, as is your business partner, and your two personalities and characteristics combine.

Here are some considerations to discuss to create the joint Business Blueprint:

- Share and define a joint vision and goals
- Establish your legal and financial structure
- Develop a comprehensive business plan
- Establish efficient operations and processes
- Define, monitor, and evaluate key performance indicators
- Clarify roles and responsibilities—early on
- Communication and conflict resolution
- Compatibility of work ethics and values
- Long-term compatibility and growth potential
- Embrace continuous learning
- Conduct thorough market research
- Conduct due diligence
- Build a strong team
- Develop a marketing strategy

Your business blueprint and your business will develop over time, and if you have not started, run, or grown a business before, please learn before you start.

The culture you create is pervasive, and as attributed to Peter Drucker, "Culture eats strategy for breakfast." Your combined culture has a significant impact on the success or failure of strategic initiatives within a company.

> *Remember:* have the conversations upfront; it is far easier than halfway through, and if you cannot have the conversations up front, do not get into business.

"Anything good is worth waiting for." Patience and perseverance are definitely two traits for business, and they are often rewarded with something valuable and worthwhile. Be aware that in a world that thrives on instant gratification, this reminder encourages you to embrace delayed gratification and appreciate the process of achieving your goals and finding the right partner.

The journey towards something meaningful often requires time, effort, and resilience. By recognising that good things take time, you can appreciate the waiting, trusting that your patience will ultimately lead to the fulfilment of your vision.

Success in business is all about making connections. It's about forming relationships and nurturing them over time.

–Richard Branson

Your Money Blueprint

Your money blueprint serves as a guide, much like a roadmap, that shapes your thoughts, attitudes, and habits when it comes to money. It influences the way you spend, save, and envision your financial future.

It's important to take a moment and reflect on your current spending habits, considering where they originate from. Are you spending money to impress others? Have you inherited certain financial behaviours from your parents?

By examining these questions, you can gain a deeper understanding of your financial blueprint and take steps towards positive change.

Here are some actionable steps you can take to transform your money blueprint and pave the way for a better financial future:

- **Identify limiting beliefs**: Reflect on any negative beliefs or attitudes you may have about money. These beliefs can hold you back from reaching your full financial potential. Challenge and reframe these limiting beliefs to align with a more positive and abundant mindset.

- **Set clear financial goals**: Define what you want to achieve financially, whether it's saving for a deposit on a property, starting a business, or becoming debt-free. Having clear goals provides focus and direction for your financial decisions and actions.

- **Create a budget**: Develop a budget that aligns with your goals and helps you track your income and expenses. By knowing exactly where your money is going, you can identify areas where you can cut back and allocate more towards your financial objectives.

- **Cultivate mindful spending habits**: Be conscious of your spending choices and ask yourself if a purchase aligns with your values and priorities. Avoid impulsive spending and make intentional decisions that support your long-term financial goals.

- **Invest in financial education**: Continuously educate yourself about personal finance and investment strategies. Attend workshops, read books, and seek advice from reputable sources. The more knowledgeable you become, the better equipped you will be to make informed financial decisions.

- **Surround yourself with positive influences**: Surround yourself with individuals who have a healthy relationship with money and share similar financial goals. Their positive habits and attitudes can inspire and motivate you on your own financial journey.

- **Practice gratitude and abundance**: Cultivate a mindset of gratitude for what you currently have and acknowledge the abundance that exists in your life. This mindset shift can help you attract more financial opportunities and create a sense of contentment along the way.

Changing your financial blueprint is a gradual process that requires consistent effort and self-reflection. By being proactive and taking intentional steps towards positive change, you can reshape your relationship with money and create a better financial future for yourself.

Define Couple's Money Blueprint

Managing money as a couple can be a source of conflict in relationships, especially if one of you is a saver and the other a spender, or even harder if you are both spenders! It is crucial to have open and honest conversations about your financial blueprint and collaborate on managing, spending, and saving money.

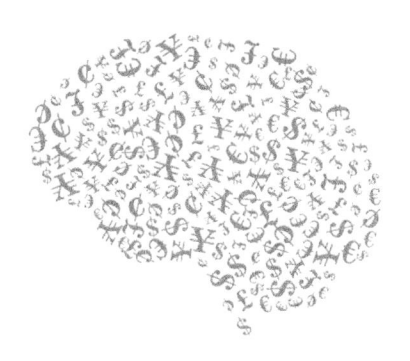

Here are three simple steps to help you define your couple's money blueprint and avoid financial disagreements:

- **Share your money blueprint ideas with your partner**: It's crucial to have an open and honest discussion about your financial situation with your partner. Sit down together and explain your money blueprint, including why it's important to make some changes and what you believe you should do as a couple to ensure your financial stability. Allow your partner to share their input and give them enough time to think and express their ideas. It is important not to impose your ideas on them; instead, work together to find common ground. If your partner already has good money habits, ask them where they learnt them and if they can share some tips to help you both improve your financial habits.

- **Agree on your financial goals**: After sharing your money blueprint ideas with your partner, it's important to agree on your financial goals as a couple. Take time to discuss and ask questions such as "What do we want in our future?" or "What is our financial goal together?" Having a common goal of becoming financially secure will provide a foundation for working together. Once you both agree on your financial goals, consider your partner's suggestions on how to reach those goals. Even if you already have a plan in place, your partner may bring up new and creative ideas that you haven't considered before. Be open-minded and willing to listen to your partner's suggestions.

- **Set up a system for managing money**: Now that you and your partner have discussed various ways to achieve your financial goals, it's time to establish a system for managing your money. To ensure the success of your plans, it is essential to be specific when creating and implementing them. For example, if your decision is to reduce your expenses, agree on precisely where you will cut back. Instead of just saying you need to trim your lifestyle expenses, be precise. It may be that you both agree to limit yourselves to eating out only once a month and that you set a specific budget, which may mean that you only order a main meal with a drink instead of a three-course meal. The more specific your plans are, the easier it will be to make decisions when it comes to implementing them.

Powerful Tips for Financial Success

If the thought of creating great wealth in terms of having a healthy bank account seems daunting to you, let's break it down into smaller tips that you can introduce into your life to help you in your pursuit of financial success:

- **Take ownership of your money**: Do not sit back and wait for someone else to give you the success you want. Instead, take charge of your own fate by making the mindset change that you are capable of creating the life you desire. By doing this, you will put yourself on the fast track to creating the wealth you desire, as you will constantly seek out ways to get you closer to your financial goals.
- **Create the right roots**: If you want to change your financial situation, you can't expect to simply continue doing the same things you have always done. Instead, you should take some time to consider your goals and work out the precise steps you need to take to get closer to them. Make sure you build the correct roots and nurture them properly to bear the financial fruits you want to produce.
- **Get comfortable with being uncomfortable**: One of the reasons why many people fail to reach the financial success they want is because they stay in their comfort zone for too long. If you are willing to step out of your comfort zone and become comfortable with feeling uncomfortable, you can put yourself on a path to creating success you may not have thought would be possible. Being uncomfortable is a sign that you are challenging yourself and putting yourself in a position where you can grow and learn.

- **Break the habit of complaining**: If you are constantly moaning about everything that may seem wrong in your life, you are creating a negative mindset. This will result in you focusing too much of your time and attention on the negative aspects of your life, which will then result in you getting negative results and not reaching your financial goals. Focus only on aspects that will help you improve your life, as this will help propel you to the financial success you desire.
- **Follow through on decisions**: You may constantly start projects and not complete them on time. This can affect the level of success that you create, as you may start to doubt your own ability to follow through on decisions and projects. The more you follow through on your decisions and complete all tasks that you start, the more you will feel confident in your own ability to complete any task you take on. This "can-do" attitude can push you closer to reaching your goals.
- **Learn to manage your money**: You need to become deliberate and make conscious decisions about every penny that you spend. While we have already discussed the importance of creating and sticking to a monthly budget, let's recap some of the steps you can take:

1. Create automated savings to make sure money is sent to your savings account before you start paying your bills.

2. Divide your savings for specific purposes, such as a vacation and an emergency fund. Make sure your emergency fund is in an account where you have easy access to the money but cannot simply swipe a card to use it.

3. Make sure you make sufficient provisions for your retirement. This is vital! Imagine being old and on the breadline!

> **Remember**: The earlier you start, the greater the compound effect will be.

4. Delay all big purchases by at least a few days to ensure you don't waste money on buying things you don't really need.

5. Review your budget and spending frequently so that you are aware of overspending on certain items and can adjust your spending in time.

6. Pay off your credit card debt as soon as possible and avoid taking out high-interest loans. If you do need to get access to more funds, make sure you accept the lowest interest rate possible.

7. Make sure you pay your bills on time to avoid late penalties and to keep your credit record as healthy as possible.

- **Never limit your income**: When you work for a company, you may feel that your income is limited to your salary. However, this does not have to be the case. There are various ways you can supplement your income. If you can't think of ways to do this, look online for possibilities for things you can do. Also, consider the possibility of creating a recurring income. Another way to remove any limitations on your income is by starting your own business. Consider how your skills can fill a gap in the market and what you will need to do to be successful.

Remember: If you don't know what you don't know, then you don't know what you don't know. So, what don't you know?"

- **Focus on solutions**: Many people are focused predominantly on how much money they can make, which can divert their attention from what they need to do to reach the success they desire. Change this by focusing on using your skills effectively to provide solutions to problems. Once you make a habit of coming up with solutions, you will set yourself up to become an unstoppable force, whether for the company you work for or within your own business.
- **Always be ready to learn**: If you are constantly looking for opportunities to learn and turn any difficulties you may experience along the way into chances to learn, you will make sure you are on the road to the success you desire. The more you are willing to learn, the more you will grow and the closer you will get to reaching your goals.

The Cashflow Quadrant

The cashflow quadrant is a valuable tool that provides insights into your income generation and wealth creation strategies while helping you minimise your tax burden. It classifies individuals into four distinct categories based on their primary source of income. Understanding these categories allows you to explore opportunities for increasing your income and building wealth more effectively. By identifying which quadrant, you currently fall into and by gaining knowledge about the other quadrants, you can make informed decisions to move towards your financial freedom and success (Robert Kiyosaki, 1998):

4. **The Investor Cruise Ship**: This cruise ship represents being an investor, where you put your money to work for you. You're a passenger on this ship, enjoying the journey while your investments generate income and appreciate in value. Your money works tirelessly for you, creating wealth and recurring income streams.

Now that you have a grasp of the four categories, this is how you move from one to the other, and each time you move forward, you increase your ability to become financially free and create long-term financial security.

- **Employee Boat to Self-Employed Canoe**: Transitioning from the employee boat to the self-employed canoe is a step towards taking control of your income. As an employee, you trade time for money, and your earning potential is limited by a fixed salary or hourly wage. By becoming self-employed, you start a business or offer services where you have more control over your income. You can set your rates, determine your working hours, and have the potential to earn more based on your efforts.

- **Self-Employed Canoe to Business Yacht**: While being self-employed offers more control and higher earning potential, it often requires your constant involvement. To achieve financial freedom, you need to transition from being self-employed to owning a business that can operate independently of your day-to-day involvement. By building systems, delegating tasks, and hiring a team, you can create a business that generates income even when you're not personally working. This allows you to leverage the efforts of others and scale your business to new heights.

- **Business Yacht to Investor Cruise Ship**: As a business owner, you have control and the potential for significant income. However, the key to long-term wealth is transitioning from the active income generated by your business to recurring income through investing. By wisely investing your profits and building a diversified portfolio, you can create multiple streams of income. These investments can include real estate, stocks, bonds, mutual funds, and other assets that appreciate in value or generate consistent returns. Over time, your investments can generate enough recurring income to sustain your lifestyle without the need for active work.

Moving through these transitions allows you to create wealth and achieve financial freedom. Each step brings you closer to a life where your money works for you rather than you having to work for your money. By diversifying your income streams, leveraging the efforts of others, and making smart investment decisions, you can build a solid foundation for financial independence. Ultimately, the goal is to reach the investor cruise ship, where your investments generate sufficient income to support your desired lifestyle, giving you the freedom to enjoy your time and pursue your passions. By understanding the different boats or vehicles, you can evaluate your current situation and decide where you want to be. The goal is to transition from the employee or self-employed quadrant into the business and investor quadrants, where you have more control, freedom, and the potential for exponential growth.

If you are on the left side of the quadrant—employed or self-employed—typically, you will struggle more financially than those on the right side, despite thinking that you have some sort of security in your financial life. However, in reality, when you choose security over calculated risks, you will find it very hard to achieve the financial freedom you desire. You will most likely pay higher taxes and be offered higher-interest rate loans to make your purchases.

To create *Wealth Beyond Money*, you will need to move from the left side of the cashflow quadrant to the right. To do this, you need to increase your financial intelligence by understanding that the amount of money you earn does not make you wealthy, but rather the amount of money you can keep and use to earn money through either recurring income or long-term capital appreciation.

Moving from the left to the right side of this cash flow quadrant is, therefore, all about changing how you view business and investment compared to the presumed security and certainty of being employed or self-employed. Adopting the following three changes in your life can make a big difference in the success of your financial future:

- Have a long-term plan and vision for how you want your financial future to look.

- Practice delayed gratification as much as you can by waiting before you indulge or spend your money.

- Learn to use compounding to your advantage. We will discuss this in more detail in Chapter 13.

Moving from the left to the right of the quadrant is all about making certain changes to go from living pay cheque to pay cheque to using some of your money to invest wisely to develop and earn a recurring income. Even if you do not have a lot of money to invest, start out small and gradually increase your investment portfolio by compounding your money. Over time, you will see your investment grow.

Very simply, the path to the right side of the quadrant starts with thinking in terms of acquiring assets that produce capital appreciation, recurring income, or business value rather than living in a pattern of pay cheque to pay cheque. Start small, have patience, and watch as your wealth grows over time.

An employee or self-employed person can start a business by using their salary to cover the initial costs and gradually building it on the side. Simultaneously, you can set aside a portion of your earnings to invest in opportunities like stocks, real estate, or other asset classes, thus becoming an investor. By managing your finances wisely and leveraging your current income, you can expand your financial horizons and work towards your business and investment goals.

Cashflow Quadrant and the 21st Century

In today's digital age, with the worldwide access and power of the internet, the opportunity to have one or more recurring income streams has never been easier. This, combined with the advancements in artificial intelligence, has opened up unparalleled opportunities to create income, businesses, or side hustles, all while maintaining your regular job. It has never been easier to embark on a journey towards financial independence and fulfilment. Children as young as nine are becoming multi-millionaires.

Harnessing the potential of this ever-changing technology requires a mindset fuelled by curiosity, determination, creativity, and a willingness to adapt. The internet provides a world of choice that can help you transform your passions, skills, and knowledge into profitable ventures. Whether through e-commerce, affiliate marketing, content creation, or offering online services, the options are virtually limitless.

One of the most empowering aspects of this new paradigm is the accessibility it offers. You no longer need expensive physical infrastructure or a large capital investment to start your own venture. With just a computer or smartphone and an internet connection, you can build an online presence, connect with a global audience, and generate a steady income stream.

Embracing this path requires a proactive approach. It is crucial to stay abreast of the latest trends, technologies, and strategies relevant to your chosen field. Engage in continuous learning, seeking out resources, courses, and communities that can help you enhance your skills and expand your horizons.

> *Remember*: Success in the digital world thrives on agility and adaptability.

While building a recurring-income business or side hustle may take time and effort, the rewards are immeasurable. Imagine having the freedom to work on your terms, pursue your passions, and control your financial destiny. The internet and AI have levelled the playing field, allowing anyone with dedication and a growth mindset to achieve remarkable results.

Here are five common examples of recurring income businesses:

1. **E-commerce**: With the rise of online shopping, starting an ecommerce business has become an attractive option. Whether you choose to sell physical products or digital goods, platforms like Shopify, Etsy, or Amazon allow you to set up an online store with relative ease. By leveraging drop shipping, print-on-demand services, or creating your own products, you can generate recurring income from repeat customers.

2. **Affiliate Marketing**: This business model revolves around promoting products or services others offer and earning a commission for each sale made through your referral. By building a niche website, a blog, or leveraging social media platforms, you can recommend products you genuinely believe in and in turn earn recurring income when people purchase through your unique affiliate links.

3. **Online Courses and Digital Products**: If you possess specialised knowledge or skills in a particular field, you can create and sell online courses, eBooks, templates, or other digital products. Platforms like Udemy, Teachable, or Gumroad provide the infrastructure to reach a global audience and generate recurring income as people enrol in your courses or purchase your digital products.

4. **Subscription-based Services**: Offering subscription-based services is another effective way to establish recurring income. This can include anything from software-as-a-service (SaaS) products, membership sites, exclusive content subscriptions, or coaching and consulting services. By providing ongoing value and maintaining customer satisfaction, you can build a loyal subscriber base that continues to pay for your services.

5. **Content Creation**: The demand for engaging and informative content is on the rise. By creating compelling videos on platforms like YouTube, hosting a podcast, or writing a blog, you can monetise your content through advertising, sponsorships, or by offering premium content to your audience. Over time, as your audience grows, your recurring income can increase through ad revenue, brand partnerships, or Patreon subscriptions.

These are just a few examples, and the possibilities are vast. The key is to find a niche that aligns with your interests, skills, and expertise, and then leverage the power of the internet and AI to scale your recurring income business or side hustle.

> *Remember*: With dedication, perseverance, and a commitment to providing value, you can turn your passion into a sustainable source of income while enjoying the flexibility and freedom that comes with it.

Embrace the power of the internet and AI, unlock your potential, and you can create a recurring income business or side hustle that supports your lifestyle and brings you joy, satisfaction, and freedom.

CHAPTER 10:
Health Is Wealth

You have most likely heard all your life that you should take care of your health, however do you truly know what great health really means? We all have our own visual idea or notion of what being in good health means. These ideas will have been greatly impacted by the health blueprints we grew up with.

To create *Wealth Beyond Money*, it is important that you relook at your ideas and previous health blueprints to make sure you are not just working on avoiding getting sick or feeling weak.

You should work on all three spheres of health: physical, mental, and emotional.

Good health helps you live a full life and create the lifestyle that you have always desired.

Take a look at your current life and health. Are you making good choices that will bring you closer to achieving optimal health? What unhealthy habits do you still have that you need to break? What changes do you need to make to your health blueprint? If you struggle with determining what changes you need to make, we will now discuss all three spheres of your overall health.

Benefits of a Healthy Life

Working on improving your health will bring many benefits on a physical, mental, and emotional level. To gain optimal health, it is important that you take a holistic approach so that you do not simply work on only one aspect of your health but make sure you create a blueprint that will address every aspect of your health to gain maximum benefits. Some of these benefits include:

- **Adds a spark to your sex life**: When you are out of shape or if you lack energy, your libido may be affected. If you work on improving your health, you may enjoy physical intimacy a lot more and feel more confident in bed, which will boost your sex life. Regular physical exercise may even improve your sexual performance. It can result in women getting more aroused, and erectile dysfunction is more common among men who are not physically active.

- **Boosts energy**: Being physically active will boost your energy levels, which will make working hard on your tasks to reach your various goals a lot easier. It will also improve your endurance, which will help you stay on task longer.

- **Reduces stress**: While you are exercising, your body will release many endorphins and hormones that will make you feel good about yourself. While these feel-good hormones are being released, your body's natural release of cortisol, the stress hormone, will be reduced, resulting in you experiencing less stress.

- **Improves mood**: As mentioned above, your body releases many feel-good hormones and endorphins while you are working out. This can help improve your mood, leaving you feeling happier and more content with who you are.

- **Promotes better sleep**: Being more physically active during the day will boost your body's release of melatonin, the hormone that helps you fall asleep at night. This will help you create better sleeping habits and wake up the next day feeling refreshed. Just make sure you do not exercise too close to bedtime, as this can result in a delayed production of melatonin.

- **Weight management**: Taking care of your health will help you manage your weight more effectively. Eating healthy meals will result in your body burning fat to create energy, and exercising will boost this even more.

- **Prevents falls**: Being more physically active will help you become more flexible and move with more ease. This can help you prevent falls and injuries. This is especially important as you get older, as falls can result in serious injuries and fractures that may even be fatal.

- **Reduces the risk of chronic ailments**: Improving your overall health, both internally and externally, will help you reduce the risk of many chronic conditions and disabilities, and may even decrease the severity of existing ailments. Some of the medical conditions that are known to be improved by a healthier lifestyle include:

- cardiovascular disease
- strokes
- type 2 diabetes and metabolic syndromes
- arthritis, high blood pressure, anxiety, and depression
- some cancers, such as bladder, breast, oesophagus, kidney, lung, stomach,

- **Strengthens your bones and muscles**: When you give your body healthy, nutritious food and become more physically active, the health of your bones, muscles, and joints will also improve.

Boost Your Physical Health

Your physical health is all about how well your body is doing in terms of fitness, diet, and nutrition. A well-balanced diet with regular exercise can make a person happy and fit and reduce fatigue, depression, and lethargy. A diet full of refined, unhealthy, and poor food choices can lead to several health risks, such as high cholesterol, an increase in blood sugar, obesity, cardiovascular diseases, and diabetes.

To boost your physical health, start by following a healthy lifestyle. This means eating a well-balanced diet and avoiding overeating or indulging in junk food, oils, added sugars, refined flour, and processed foods. Instead, focus on consuming nutritious foods like whole grains, legumes, vegetables, fruits, and nuts. A Mediterranean diet, rich in these wholesome foods, can be beneficial. It includes lean sources of protein like fish and poultry and moderate consumption of red wine.

In addition to making good food choices, the evidence from controlled studies highlights that regular, moderate exercise is crucial for keeping your body in shape, increasing your energy levels, and making you feel active. Aim for at least 30 to 60 minutes of moderate exercise each day. Even 15 minutes of vigorous exercise can have a positive impact.

If you've neglected your physical health for a while, making changes might seem overwhelming. However, breaking it down into smaller, more achievable tasks can make it easier to reach your goals. Here's how you can do it:

- **Build healthy habits**: Identify unhealthy habits in your life and consider replacing them with healthier alternatives. This could include quitting smoking, reducing alcohol consumption, avoiding excessive sitting, or cutting back on unhealthy foods. Introduce healthier habits like drinking four large glasses of water every day, choosing nutritious snacks when hungry, and practicing daily gratitude to boost your overall well-being and help you feel better about yourself.

- **Eat a healthy diet**: Ensure that the majority of the food you consume is nutritious and supports your physical health. Overindulging in unhealthy options not only puts your physical health at risk but also affects your mental and emotional well-being.

- **Get active**: If you have a sedentary lifestyle, you can reduce the risk of medical problems by becoming more physically active. Apart from regular workouts, make small changes in your daily routine, like taking a longer route to the bathroom, using stairs instead of elevators, or sitting on a yoga ball while watching television.

- **Get proper rest**: A good night's sleep is crucial for your overall health. Create a sleep-friendly environment by ensuring your room is dark and cool. Avoid screens for at least an hour before bed to promote better sleep. Establish a consistent sleep routine by going to bed at the same time each night.

- **Practice self-care**: Take care of yourself by being aware of when you need a break and practicing self-care. If you neglect self-care, it can impact your ability to accomplish tasks and negatively affect your mental and emotional health.

By prioritising your physical health and incorporating these steps into your life, you can enhance your overall well-being and create a healthier future for yourself.

Remember: small changes over time can make a significant difference in your physical health and overall happiness.

Love Your Mental Health

We can all have good mental health 100% of the time, and importantly, without good mental health, life becomes more difficult. As a concept, mental health is generally spoken about negatively.

For the majority of you, mental health is in your control, and when you lose control, it can become a hindrance by causing feelings of frustration, aggression, depression, anxiety, stress, and suicidal ideations. Mental health is as important or even more important than physical health. Monitor and maintain it as you would your physical being.

Remember: You cannot see mental health, and it has an enormous impact on you, recognise quickly if it begins to slide.

Be aware of your mind and how it is thinking; listen to it, and it will let you know when it requires more attention. When you become aware of signs that your mental health is starting to slide, immediately act and practice self-care activities to reduce any restrictive or negative feelings you may have. Self-care can include meditation, practicing mindfulness, doing yoga, breathing deeply, or even a simple walk outdoors to reduce stress.

Remember: Diet, hydration, sleep, and exercise play a big part in maintaining good mental health.

Let's look at more ways you can do this:

- **Positive attitude towards life**: Always seek out the positives in every situation you may find yourself in. It is helpful to create a habit of practicing gratitude, whereby you name and appreciate something you are grateful for every day. This can be something as simple as being grateful for having a warm bed to sleep in or something bigger, such as being grateful that you have your health, an income, and your relationships, or that you are in a position to adopt philanthropic activities. There is always good in every situation; sometimes, you just need to find it.
- **Being happy and sharing happiness**: Surround yourself with positive people who you can share your happiness with and who can pick you up on days you are feeling down, depressed, anxious, or defeated. A simple rule to follow: wake up, smile, and say, "I am happy." It works wonders on all days.

- **Accept failures**: Life is not perfect; no one is perfect, and there will be times when you make mistakes. It is life's learning that creates wisdom. If you start knowing this will happen, it lessens the impact when it does. This is not negative; it is a pragmatic approach, especially when you are doing things differently. You will bounce back a lot quicker if you seek out the positives in life. When you do have an off day, accept it, and manage it without allowing it to let you fall out of balance.
- **Be creative**: Finding creativity in life can be a fantastic tool for improving your mental health. Think about what you enjoy doing that is creative. This can be painting a picture, making something, working in the garden, or even just doodling on a sheet of paper. This can be extremely helpful in calming yourself and making you feel good about yourself.

- **Keep learning**: Humans have evolved to adapt and change constantly in response to their environment. Committing to lifelong learning is one of the best ways to ensure this evolution and growth continue. Seeking out opportunities to learn and improve your abilities not only helps you avoid feelings of complacency and defeat but also provides you with a sense of accomplishment and confidence as you tackle new challenges. Embrace the power of lifelong learning and prioritise it in your life—whether it's taking a course, learning a new skill, or exploring a new topic, your wisdom increases.
- **Spend time in nature**: Spend as much time in nature as possible; this will boost your body's release of dopamine, a feel-good hormone. Take a walk through nature, barefoot if you can, to connect to the earth's power, or sit outside in the fresh air as frequently as you can, even if it is just having your cup of coffee or tea outside in the sun during a break from routine activities, whatever they may be. Nature helps to reduce stress and promote relaxation, and of course, nature allows us to disconnect from the hustle and bustle of daily life and connect with the natural world around us, providing a much-needed break for our body and mind.

- **Connect with others**: Positive social connections and relationships provide support and a sense of belonging and reduce feelings of loneliness or isolation. Engaging in activities that bring joy and a sense of purpose, such as hobbies, volunteering, or creative pursuits. Beware of negative comparison: It is important to remember that each person's journey is unique, and negatively comparing yourself to others can be detrimental as it can lead to dissatisfaction and a lowering of self-esteem. Recognise that connection and belonging are fundamental human needs, and if you find yourself isolating, take proactive steps to change course before it takes a toll on your overall mental health.

- **Feeling angry?** This could be a signal that your boundaries have been crossed.

- **Feeling sad?** Perhaps something valuable has been lost.

- **Feeling grateful?** You are appreciating and valuing something you have or admire.

- **Feeling frustrated?** Harness that energy to drive you forward.

- **Feeling happy?** Share the joy and positivity in your interactions with others.

It is okay to feel anything you do; it is what you do with the feeling that counts. By acknowledging and understanding the messages your emotions deliver, you can use them to increase self-awareness and personal growth.

Do not suppress or ignore your emotions; instead, listen to them. Avoidance is not mastery. As uncomfortable as some feelings may be, their acknowledgement allows you to discover and address the root cause, leading to resolution and growth when you choose that option.

However, while it's crucial to honour and understand your emotions, it is equally essential not to let them dictate your actions blindly. Emotional intelligence is vital to develop because it provides the capacity to manage and respond to your emotions appropriately. Being angry doesn't necessitate an outburst, just as feeling fearful doesn't always require avoidance. You can recognise your emotions without being ruled by them.

Finally, practice makes progress. Emotional mastery is a journey, not a destination. Mindfulness, the practice of paying attention to your thoughts and feelings without judging them, is an invaluable tool for mastering your emotions. When you become an observer of your emotional state, you identify patterns and triggers. This self-awareness creates a space for choice.

In essence, the power of emotions is immense. Mastering them doesn't mean eradicating or controlling them, but rather understanding, honouring, and intelligently responding to them, and there lies true emotional mastery.

Raising your Emotional Intelligence (EI) and Emotional Quotient (EQ) and applying the knowledge to your life will help you in every walk of life you traverse.

Remember: You have the power to harness your emotions for your greater good.

Enhance Your Social Health

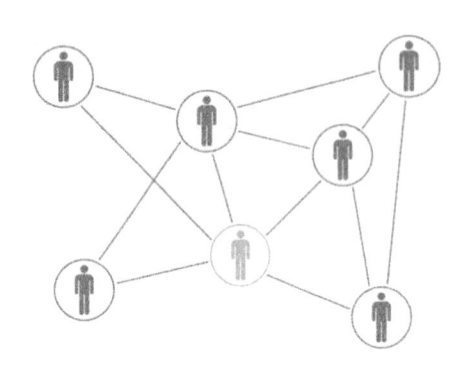

Social health's power lies in connecting with others and building positive, fulfilling relationships. When you surround yourself with supportive, uplifting people, you create a network of love and support that can tremendously impact your overall health and well-being. However, it is important to be mindful of who we allow into our lives—sadly, not everyone has your best interests at heart. Negative relationships do occur and can have a devastating effect on your well-being.

Your network creates a culture that you operate within when you accept the culture that the interactions create. If your current network is not providing you with what you require, then change is a must. It sounds harsh, and it is the truth. Who you interact with is a choice you make intentionally to achieve your primary values in life and your vision. Now, many visions are unconscious! Think about what you want to achieve and focus your learning and connections in that direction.

Remember: It is said that you are the sum of the five people you spend the most time associating with.

Are the five people with whom you spend most of your time having a good or bad influence on you?

Let's look at some tips on how to improve your social health:

- **Build Relationships**: Cultivate positive relationships with family, friends, colleagues, and your community. Invest time and effort into developing meaningful connections. Participate in social activities, join clubs, communities, networks, or groups with shared interests, and make an effort to meet new people. Participate in social activities and join groups with shared interests both offline and online—the world is a wide-open resource.

- **Choose the culture**: Identify the environment you want to spend time in and avoid the environmental and personal cultures that do not fit your choice. Look for positive influence, growth, joy, and connection. It is out there, and remember, it is your choice to be in all relationships; you can stay, change, or leave. Leaving will be one of the best decisions you make on occasions.

- **Know yourself**: Being self-aware and true to yourself has numerous benefits: It enhances your confidence and self-esteem, and you make more authentic choices that align with your values and beliefs. It enables you to establish and maintain healthy boundaries, make assertive decisions, and build more genuine and meaningful relationships. It allows you to respond to life's challenges with greater clarity and resilience.

- **Active Participation**: We are not all blessed with family or friends; therefore, engaging actively in social activities is vital to our overall health. Remember, solitude and isolation are different, creating different needs and wants. You can volunteer and engage in social events that align with your interests and values. Active participation increases your sense of belonging and fulfilment. It can also build a supportive and encouraging network.

- **Improve Communication skills**: Effective communication is essential for building and maintaining strong relationships and is a key skill to develop both orally and in writing. Focus on active listening, expressing yourself clearly, and being empathetic towards others. Good communication helps in understanding others, resolving conflicts, and building deeper connections. Discover *The Leadership Voice Programme* at JulieHogbin.com.

- **Leverage Positive Affirmations and Afformations**: Utilise affirmations, and personal declarations of truth, to bolster your self-belief and potential. Simultaneously, afformations, structured as uplifting questions, direct your mind towards positivity and personal growth. Together, these tools create a robust mindset and mindflow that accelerate your transformation and goal attainment.

While boosting your social health will help you improve your overall health, it will also help you create meaningful relationships and find balance in your life.

Remember: Social health is a lifelong journey that requires ongoing effort and attention. Everything changes over time.

CHAPTER 11:
Creating Meaningful Relationships

The quality of your life is the quality of your relationships.
−**Tony Robbins**

To create true *Wealth Beyond Money*, you need to work on your health, your relationships, and your finances. The quality of your life is dependent on the calibre of your relationships, both with yourself and others.

The most important relationship you will ever have—is with yourself. The importance of your internal dialogue is key to understanding how that affects you, both positively and negatively, as well as your interactions with others. No one ever does anything on their own. You are always supported by others, implicitly and explicitly.

People come into your life for three main purposes: a reason, a season, or a lifetime. It is up to you to decide how long people will stay in your life, what influence they will have on you, and your ability to achieve your goals. Some people will encourage and motivate you to move forward in life, while others may keep you back. This is why it is so important to determine which relationships bring value and balance to your life and do what you can to nurture them. To help you create the perfect blueprint for relationships in your life, we will now discuss not only how to build healthy relationships with yourself and others but also the value of creating solid connections in business and setting healthy boundaries to protect yourself and your relationships.

Basis of a Healthy Relationship

Before we delve into ways to improve your relationships, let's first explore the fundamental elements that form the basis of a healthy and fulfilling connection. Take a moment to reflect on your own relationships and identify which of these critical aspects are present and where you might need to focus your efforts:

- **Care**: When you enter into a relationship with someone, caring for their well-being and ensuring their safety and security becomes a priority. Genuine care and concern lay the foundation for a strong and nurturing bond.

- **Equality**: Treating your partner as an equal is crucial. Every individual in the relationship should be valued and respected, fostering a sense of fairness and balance. In turn, you should also expect to be treated with the same level of respect and equality.

- **Honesty**: Open and honest communication is the lifeblood of any successful relationship. Transparency and truthfulness create trust and deepen the connection. Without honesty, a relationship cannot thrive or bring harmony to your life.

- **Support**: A healthy relationship involves mutual support during both good and challenging times. Being there for each other, offering encouragement, and helping one another reach their full potential strengthens the bond and nurtures personal growth.

- **Respect**: Respecting one another is essential in any relationship. It's crucial to recognise the inherent worth and value of both yourself and your partner. By treating each other with respect, you create an environment where love and understanding can flourish.

- **Trust**: Trust is the cornerstone of a healthy relationship. Building and maintaining trust requires reliability, consistency, and integrity. Without trust, the relationship becomes fragile and unstable.

- **Understanding**: Striving to understand your partner is key to fostering a deep connection. Actively listen to their thoughts and feelings without jumping to conclusions or making assumptions. Seek to comprehend their perspective before seeking to be understood yourself.

By focusing on these core elements, you can strengthen your relationships and lay the groundwork for a profound and lasting connection.

Remember: Building a healthy relationship is an ongoing process that requires commitment, effort, and a genuine desire to grow together.

Embrace these principles and watch as your relationships flourish and bring joy and fulfilment to your life.

Maintain a Healthy Relationship with Your Partner

A successful relationship requires falling in love many times, always with the same person.
                                                            –Mignon McLaughlin

A wise man once said, "If you do not want there to be an end to your relationship, do all the things throughout the relationship that you did at the beginning of the relationship, and there will be no end to the relationship." This insightful quote emphasises the importance of continuously nurturing your relationship, fostering love, and ensuring its longevity.

Embrace the proven principles on how to maintain and continually grow a loving, healthy, and fulfilling bond with your partner:

- **Cherish the present**: Instead of dwelling on past mistakes, focus on the present moment and embrace the joy you share with your partner. By letting go of past grievances, you create space for new possibilities and strengthen your connection.

- **Embrace forgiveness**: When misunderstandings or mistakes occur, be willing to offer genuine apologies and extend forgiveness. This compassionate approach fosters understanding, encourages growth, and deepens your emotional bond.

- **Detachment**: Detachment is letting go of attachment to outcomes and accepting our lack of control over others. It brings inner peace and healthier relationships by focusing on your own actions instead.

- **Letting go**: Letting go means consciously choosing to release resentments, grudges, and past hurts. It involves freeing yourself from the emotional baggage that weighs you down, allowing you to experience greater peace and personal growth.

- **Shower affection**: Demonstrate your love and appreciation for your partner by expressing affection in meaningful ways. Small gestures, such as hugs, kisses, and kind words, and making them feel special will create an ongoing warm and loving atmosphere.

- **Communicate openly**: Foster clear and open communication with your partner. Express your desires, needs, and concerns honestly while also attentively listening to their thoughts and feelings. Effective communication builds trust and strengthens your emotional connection.

- **Discover new adventures**: Continually seek out new experiences and adventures together. Exploring shared interests and trying new things injects excitement into your relationship and helps you grow together as a couple.

- **Nurture intimacy**: Cultivate a fulfilling and intimate connection with your partner. Engage in activities that nurture emotional and physical closeness, creating a safe space for vulnerability and deepening your bond.

- **Support each other's dreams**: Encourage and support your partner in pursuing their dreams and aspirations. Show genuine interest in their goals, offer encouragement, and celebrate their achievements. By nurturing individual growth, you strengthen the foundation of your relationship.

- **Practice gratitude**: Express gratitude for your partner and the love you share. Regularly acknowledge and appreciate their efforts, kindness, and presence in your life. Gratitude strengthens the positive aspects of your relationship and cultivates a sense of fulfilment and contentment.

- **Create lasting memories**: Prioritise quality time together and make meaningful memories. Engage in activities that bring you both joy and create lasting bonds, such as going on adventures, taking trips, or simply enjoying peaceful moments of togetherness. Couples that play together tend to stay together.

- **Keep the romance alive**: Infuse romance into your relationship by regularly engaging in romantic gestures, surprises, and thoughtful acts of love. Keep the flame burning by consistently showing your partner that they are loved, cherished, protected, and adored. Apart from your relationship with yourself, make your relationship with your partner your top priority. Show them daily that they are the most important person in your life.

Imagine your relationships as a savings account where you have the power to make deposits and watch them grow over time. Just like with a savings account, the initial efforts you put into building a relationship are crucial. You invest love, affection, time, and energy to ensure a strong foundation.

However, here is the important part: if you only withdraw from your relationship without making consistent deposits, eventually, your emotional savings will dwindle. Just as spending all your savings without replenishing them leads to financial hardship, neglecting to invest in your relationships can leave them depleted and devoid of love.

To keep your relationships thriving, it is vital to continue investing in them with the same passion and dedication as you did in the beginning. Keep making deposits of love, kindness, understanding, and support. Nurture your connections by actively listening, communicating openly, and showing appreciation for one another.

> *Remember*: the more you invest, the more your relationships will flourish. Just like compounding interest in a savings account, your consistent deposits of love and affection will accumulate and generate incredible returns. The bond you share with your loved ones will grow stronger, deeper, and more resilient.

It's not just about making deposits; it is also about balancing withdrawals. While it's natural to seek love, care, and support from your relationships, it's essential to reciprocate and give back in equal measure. Continually replenishing the emotional reservoirs in your relationships ensures a harmonious balance and sustains the connection you share.

Strive to maintain a healthy equilibrium by continuously depositing love, kindness, and affection while being mindful of not excessively withdrawing without replenishing. By investing consistently in your relationships, you create a cycle of love and positivity that perpetually fuels the bond you share.

The grass isn't greener on the other side, the grass is greenest where it is watered and nurtured the most!
–Neil Barringham.

Build Business Relationships

In business, relationships are everything. It's not just what you know, but who you know. They are about giving and receiving. - Bob Burg.

Building strong business relationships is crucial for creating *Wealth Beyond Money*. These relationships play a vital role in the progression of your career and financial health. As we've discussed, they also provide you with leverage options to help you achieve your goals. Let's explore ways to ensure you build solid connections in the business world:

- **Get to know the person**: Before creating strong connections, take the time to truly understand the individuals you're engaging with. Aim for longer-term relationships rather than simply connecting with the first person who approaches you. Choose your business partners as though you were employing them, considering compatibility and shared values.

- **Apply your time and resources to key social issues**: Show your business partners that you are more than just a potential network connection. Demonstrate your commitment to social causes and give back to your community. By aligning yourself with important issues, you'll build a reputation as someone who genuinely cares about making a positive impact.

- **Diversify your network**: Don't limit yourself to networking within your industry. Create connections with people from various types of businesses. Embrace diversity in your network, as it brings fresh perspectives and opportunities for collaboration.

- **Give more than you expect**: Consider what you would like to receive from your business networks, whether it's resources, time, or sharing ideas. Position yourself as someone who is willing to give back and provide value. By going above and beyond, you'll show your business connections that you're not just there to use them but to contribute to their success as well.

- **Prune, renew, and reshape your networks**: Evaluate the value that each network brings to your life and goals. If a specific network isn't beneficial, don't be afraid to limit your time and energy spent on it. Instead, focus on cultivating connections that align with your aspirations and can propel you forward.

- **Spend quality time on key relationships**: Identify the business relationships that have the potential to significantly impact your journey. Prioritise these connections and invest your time and energy in nurturing them.

Building business relationships is a dynamic process. It requires genuine effort, consistency, and a willingness to give back. By following these principles, you will forge powerful connections and cultivate a network that supports your growth and opens doors to new opportunities.

CHAPTER 12:
Power of Money

We all need and want money. Many people determine their own worth by the amount of money they have in the bank. But what is money? To put it simply, money is a human concept and invention that facilitates the distribution of tangible resources and assets. The currency we use only works if we agree on the system and play by the economic rules that create it. It is, therefore, a commodity that is accepted by general consent as a medium of economic exchange.

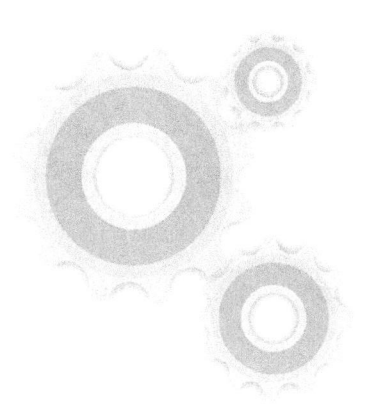

Money is typically exchanged for either time, such as getting paid to do a nine-to-five job, or a service, such as a plumber or an accountant, or for creating solutions to a problem. The bigger the problem you can solve, the more value (or money) you create. Think about companies such as Microsoft, Google, and Amazon. They saw big gaps or problems in the market and pretty much monopolised it by creating a solution.

Many people believe that you need to have money to make money. However, this is not true. Money is literally everywhere around us. You just need to know where to look and who to ask for it. There is a famous saying that is worth repeating from earlier "If you don't know what you don't know, then you don't know what you don't know. So, what don't you know?"

We live in a new world where millionaires are literally created daily due to the incredible speed and global reach of the internet, coupled with social media exposure and incredible income-generating software. Think about all the so-called social media influencers or YouTube stars that are appearing overnight, earning literally millions for creating content. What do they know that you don't?

To help you figure out how you can improve your cash flow and increase your bank account, we will now discuss the different characteristics of money and what you can do to achieve financial freedom. Then, we will discuss the power of using leverage to increase your wealth.

Characteristics of Money

Money is something we use every day to buy goods and services. But have you ever wondered how money came into existence? In the past, people did not have coins or polymer notes like we do now. They used other ways to exchange things of value.

Long ago, before money, as we currently know it existed, people relied on bartering. Bartering is when you trade one thing for another without using money. For example, if you had chickens and needed wheat, you would find someone who had wheat and wanted chickens. You would negotiate a trade and exchange your chickens for their wheat.

While bartering was useful, it had its limitations. It was not always easy to find someone who had what you wanted and wanted what you had. It was also difficult to determine the value of different items. For example, how many chickens would be equal to a bag of wheat?

To solve these challenges, people started using objects with inherent value as a form of exchange. One of the earliest forms of money was made from precious metals like silver and gold. These metals were valuable and easy to carry, making them ideal for trade. People would trade goods and services in exchange for silver or gold.

Over time, coins were introduced. These coins were made from precious metals and had a specific value assigned to them. They made trading easier because everyone agreed on the value of the coins. Instead of bartering or carrying around heavy pieces of silver or gold, people could simply exchange coins.

As societies grew and became more complex, paper money was introduced. Paper money represents a specific amount of precious metal, usually gold or silver, held by the government or a trusted institution. It was more convenient to carry and use than coins, and it allowed for larger transactions.

Today, we use polymer notes and coins as our primary form of physical currency. We no longer need to carry around precious metals for trade. Money has become a universal medium of exchange that is accepted everywhere. It makes buying and selling goods and services much easier and more efficient.

Money did once grow on trees as it was made of paper, but that is no longer the case, and it is no longer backed by gold as it once was. The money landscape has changed and is changing dramatically.

As a result, money came into existence as a way to solve the challenges of bartering and provide a common medium of exchange. It replaced other forms of exchange value like trading and bartering, as well as the use of precious metals like silver and gold:

- **Acceptability**: Money is universally accepted as a medium of exchange in transactions because it is widely recognised and valued by people everywhere. This widespread acceptance makes transactions smoother and more efficient compared to trading livestock or bartering, where the acceptability of goods or services may vary among different individuals or communities.

- **Divisibility**: Money can be divided into smaller units to accommodate different values, making it easier to exchange and trade. This divisibility of money eliminates the challenges of bartering or trading livestock, where the value of goods or animals may not align with the desired exchange, resulting in difficulties in finding suitable trades.

- **Durability**: Money is made from durable materials, ensuring that it remains in good condition over time. This durability is crucial in maintaining the value of money and enables it to be used repeatedly, unlike livestock or perishable goods that may lose value or deteriorate over time.

- **Limited supply**: The controlled supply of money helps maintain its value over time. Governments and central banks regulate the production and circulation of money to prevent inflation and preserve its purchasing power, and of course, the reverse is true: The government can print money on demand. A limited supply ensures that money retains its worth, unlike goods or livestock, which may fluctuate in value based on factors such as availability or demand.

- **Portability**: Money is lightweight and easy to carry, allowing for convenient transactions. Its portability makes it more practical compared to trading livestock or bulky goods, as money can be easily transported and used for various purchases without the need for the physical transfer of large or heavy items.

- **Uniformity**: Money is designed to have a consistent appearance and standard features, making it easily recognisable and verifiable. This uniformity eliminates the need for lengthy negotiations or evaluations that often accompany bartering or trading livestock, where the quality, condition, or authenticity of goods can be subjective and time-consuming to assess.

As a result of these characteristics, money has become a widely accepted and trusted medium of exchange, enabling people from different regions and cultures to engage in economic activities on a global scale. Money offers greater efficiency, flexibility, and ease of use in economic transactions, making it a preferred medium of exchange in modern societies.

Digitalisation and Crypto

We, as authors, cannot, not, recognise the changes that have occurred and are building in the 21st century we live in that alter our relationship with money, what we do with it, and how we do it.

Remember: Money is a made-up concept; therefore, it can be remade.

Digitalisation has brought about a fundamental shift in how money is stored, transferred, and accessed. Traditional physical currencies are being replaced by digital forms of payment, such as online banking and mobile wallets. This has made transactions faster, more convenient, and accessible to a wider range of people. However, it has also raised concerns about privacy, security, and the potential for financial exclusion. Not everyone has equal access to digital technologies or the knowledge to navigate them effectively.

Online banking, tapping for payment, digitalisation, and crypto have revolutionised the way we handle financial transactions, offering change, convenience, and efficiency. However, they have also brought about potential negative effects on people's connections to money and spending habits.

Firstly, the digitalisation of banking has led to a reduced sense of tangibility and visibility of money. In traditional cash transactions, you would physically handle money, which provides a tangible connection to your money and spending. With online banking, money can become an abstract concept represented by numbers on a screen, making it easier to lose track of your spending and overspend without realising the physical consequences.

This detachment can lead to a diminished sense of financial responsibility and a weakened connection to the value of money. Along with the ease of borrowing and credit, you can soon build up 'bad' debt. Please, we implore you to connect with your finances if you have not already. Do not lead yourself into financial stress and debt when it can be prevented.

The ease and speed of online transactions and tapping for payment methods can contribute to impulsive buying behaviour. With a simple click or tap, money can be spent without much thought or consideration at home or internationally. This convenience can lead to mindless spending, as you may make purchases without fully assessing your financial situation or evaluating the necessity of the items you are buying.

As a result, you may become disconnected from the true value of your purchases and develop a habit of overspending.

Cryptocurrencies, on the other hand, have disrupted the traditional financial landscape by introducing decentralised and digital currencies that operate independently of central banks and governments.

Cryptos like Bitcoin and Ethereum have gained significant attention and value, attracting investors and challenging the existing financial systems. They offer benefits such as lower transaction fees, faster cross-border transfers, and the potential for financial inclusion in unbanked populations. However, they also face regulatory challenges and price volatility because the blockchain provides a transparent record of all transactions.

Overall, the impact of digitalisation and cryptocurrencies on the normal world of money is complex and evolving. While they bring innovation and opportunities for financial empowerment, they also raise questions about security, privacy, equality, regulatory frameworks, and who controls them.

Remember: Maintain a healthy relationship with your finances; however, you do that in the digital age.

Achieve Financial Freedom

To master your own finances, there are important steps to follow. The first step is understanding your current income and expenditures. Mastering your finances is an important step towards achieving financial freedom. To begin, it's crucial to understand your current income and expenditures. By creating a simple monthly income and expenditure spreadsheet budget, you can get a clear idea of your spending habits and identify areas where you can make changes. Once you've done this, it's important to be disciplined and stick to your budget.

Remember that the same principles apply to your savings and investments. Keep track of your annual returns and make adjustments as needed. This will help you maximise your earnings and achieve your financial goals faster.

There are many people who want to attain financial freedom in their lives. However, most people misunderstand what this term means and get confused between being financially wealthy and being financially free.

Being financially wealthy means that you have accumulated assets, investments, and large amounts of liquid funds.

Whereas financial freedom is having an equal sum of money to cover your normal monthly expenditure with a 10-20% buffer, for most people, having £2,000-£3,000 per month would be sufficient to cover those monthly costs and for you to attain financial freedom.

Financial freedom is about your ability to control your own finances and being able to live the life you desire without stressing over your monthly bills or how you will pay for financial emergencies.

To help you achieve the financial freedom you desire, there are a number of simple steps you can take to get you closer to your goals (fully explained by Immanuel Ezekiel's book, *The 6 Steps To Financial Freedom*):

- **Track all your spending**: Start with your last six months' bank statements; this gives you a long enough timeframe to assess your overall income and spending habits. Enter the details into a spreadsheet. Once you complete this important step, you will be surprised to see exactly where you are spending all of your income.

- **Spend less**: Always look out for ways you can reduce your monthly expenses. Look at your current expenses and identify at least five areas where you can make savings. This can include changing, renegotiating, or even cancelling monthly standing orders or direct debits, streaming, mobile phone, utilities, insurance policies, and subscriptions no longer being used. Then, look at lowering your other expenditures, such as eating out once less per month to begin with and daily lunches and coffees; these small daily expenditures add up to a lot of money per month. These savings will give you additional funds from where you think you are now to work on your financial freedom.

- **Pay off debt**: Almost all debt comes at high-interest rates that you have to pay, decreasing your cash flow and the amount of money you can save every month.

- **Pay off the smallest debt first**: Once paid off, use the money you used for this debt to pay off your next smallest debt, and so on, until all debts are repaid.

- **Invest**: Investing as much money as possible will get you closer to gaining financial freedom. Even though you may not currently have the funds to create a solid investment portfolio, it is important that you start investing as soon as possible. In Chapter 13, we will discuss the magic of compounding and how you can grow a small investment into a substantial investment portfolio relatively quickly.

- **Create additional sources of income**: If your job, profession, or business is not sufficient to create the financial freedom you desire, it would be beneficial for you to look for and create an additional stream of income. With all the advancements in the internet, AI technology, and VAs, it has never been easier to create additional streams of income, which can either be all outsourced or with VAs.

- **Create Recurring Income**: This type of income source is what you create when you do the work once but keep on generating a recurring monthly income. Typical examples of recurring income can include property rentals, selling digital content, or investing in stocks.

- **Keep increasing your value**: Whether you are employed, self-employed, or a business owner, you have to keep increasing your value to your employer or customers. The effect is that you will earn more money or make your business more valuable, which will provide you with surplus funds to invest and accelerate your progress towards attaining financial freedom. What new skills can you or do you need to learn to get closer to them?

- **Set financial goals**: Think about what you would like to achieve financially and write down your goals. This can be to save for your children's education, your retirement, travelling, or starting your own business. Once you have at least five goals written down, break them down and see what small steps you can take to get closer to reaching them.

Benefits of Financial Leverage

It increases your returns, and you will generate bigger profits. An example of leverage is when you pay a 25% deposit to get 100% of a real property. The 75% becomes leverage. Therefore, if you purchase a £200,000 rental property with a £50,000 deposit, the lender gives you £150,000 for the purchase. Therefore, property leverage allows you to increase the return on your own capital investment. Leverage is an investment strategy that involves using borrowed money—specifically, borrowed capital—to increase the potential return of an investment.

The Benefits of Gearing

Leverage will undoubtedly help you acquire more assets and generate more profits, and the use of gearing can increase your return on investment substantially. We will continue with the example above of purchasing a £200,000 rental property with a 25% deposit and look at two examples of how gearing can make a difference:

- **Example A**: Assuming the property value increases by 5% per annum. Over a 10-year period, the property and your investment would have increased by £325,778. In addition, you would have also received £1,000 per calendar month in rental income. Over a 10-year period, you would receive £120,000 in rental income (£12,000 x 10 years = £120,000).

- **Example B**: If, however, you used the same £200,000 and used £50,000 as a deposit for each property to purchase four properties instead of just one property with the same rental income, this would result in ownership of 4 x £200,000 = £800,000 worth of property with a mortgage debt of £600,000. Assuming the property value increases by the same 5% per annum, over the same 10-year period, the property and your investment would have increased to £1,303,115. After taking into consideration the £600,000 mortgage debt, your overall net investment compared to the example above would be £703,115.

- In addition, you would have also received four times the rental payments of £1,000 x 12 x 4 properties = £48,000 per annum. Then, accounting for the mortgage interest payments, £150,000 x 4 x 5% = £30,000 interest per annum (this assumes a 5% interest-only mortgage). The gross rental income is £12,000 x 4 = £48,000 less the mortgage payment interest of £30,000 above (£48,000 - £30,000 = £18,000), which would generate a net income of £18,000 per annum. Over the same 10-year period, you would receive £180,000 (£18,000 x 10 = £180,000) in rental income on the four properties. This equates to £60,000 more in rental income over the same 10-year period.

By practicing gearing, example B could make you a full £457,337 more money over the same period of time than example A would. Below is a full explanation of the sum:

Investment in example A	
Initial property value of £200,000	
Value after 10 years	£325,778
10 years rental income of £12,000 per annum	£120,000
Total amount	**£425,778**
Investment in example B	
Initial property value of £800,000	
Value after 10 years	£1,303,115
10 year rental income: £18,000 per annum	£480,000
Gross total investment	£1,783,115
Less mortgages	£600,000
Less mortgage payments	£300,000
Total net return	**£883,115**
Increase in net return:	
£883,115 – £425,778	£457,337

The example above shows a more than 100% higher return for a like-for-like investment by utilising the power of gearing. This strategy has been extensively used to generate financial wealth and income from property investments.

An example of how banks apply gearing as well as create money out of thin air: You deposit £1,000 into the bank. Firstly, it is not a deposit. It is actually a loan that you are providing to the bank. That is why many banks pay a pittance of an interest rate on the deposit (or loan to the bank). The bank is then able to lend the funds in that account at a 9:1 ratio. £1,000 deposited means the bank can lend £9,000 and charge interest to the borrower of anything between 5% and 30%, depending on if it is a secured or unsecured loan. Hypothetically, if the bank pays you 1% on your funds and then lends at 5%, it is making a 400% return on your funds. You may want to take some time to digest that equation of a 400% return.

Now comes the next part, which you may not be aware of: Once the loan is made and £9,000 is deposited into either the same bank or another bank, the process starts again. Now, the bank can make a loan of £81,000 on top of the £9,000 deposited. This process keeps on going, and that is how money is created out of thin air and how banks make billions in interest.

While you may think you do not currently have the funds to gain massive returns from investments, compounding may just be the magic ingredient that you have been missing in your recipe for financial freedom. In the next chapter, we will discuss how you can do this effectively.

It is imperative that you increase your financial IQ and understand how money works and how it is generated. You have heard many times that you cannot pull money out of thin air. However, that is exactly what banks and financial institutions do. Accessing money is easy once you know the secret to finding it.

Raising your financial IQ and knowledge means improving your understanding and expertise in managing your money and making financial decisions.

Having a high financial IQ means you have a good understanding of various financial concepts, such as budgeting, saving, investing, and managing debt. It involves being knowledgeable about how money works, including concepts like interest rates, inflation, and different investment options.

By raising your financial IQ and knowledge, you become more informed and educated about personal finance. This can help you make better financial decisions and improve your overall financial well-being. For example, you might learn how to create a budget and stick to it, understand the benefits of saving and investing for the future, or develop strategies to reduce and manage debt.

Raising your financial IQ and knowledge can be achieved through various means, such as reading books, attending financial workshops or seminars, taking online courses, or seeking guidance from financial professionals. The more you learn and understand about personal finance, the better equipped you become to make informed decisions and improve your financial situation.

CHAPTER 13:
The Magic of Compounding

Compounding is one aspect that you can control that will dramatically increase the return on your investments. Return on investment includes Time, Energy, Effort, Relationship, Health, Business, and Finances.

Albert Einstein once described compound interest as the "eighth wonder of the world," saying, "He who understands it, earns it; he who doesn't, pays for it." Compound interest is when the interest one earns on a principal balance is reinvested and generates additional interest. The difference between normal interest and compound interest over the long term is immense.

Compounding Across Health, Relationships, and Finance

Compounding will not only make a massive difference in growing your investment portfolios and getting you closer to financial freedom, it will also bring benefits to your health and relationships and support you in leading a more balanced life. Working on these three aspects of your life in combination—health, relationships and finances, and will bring you the *Wealth Beyond Money* that you desire.

When you make a conscious effort to nurture your romantic relationships, you're investing in the long-term growth and strength of the connection. Compounding interest with every loving gesture, kind word, and thoughtful action builds upon the last to create a foundation of trust, intimacy, and love. Over time, this foundation becomes stronger and more resilient, creating a bond that can withstand any challenge. Make time for your partner, show them appreciation, communicate openly and honestly, and prioritise your relationship. Continue as you started by investing rather than withdrawing.

Now, think of your health. The key to compounding is doing the right thing consistently over an extended period of time. This is also a vital principle for creating good health. Every time you choose to eat healthy meals or do physical exercise, you are choosing to improve your overall health. Have you ever heard the saying, "A minute on the lips but a lifetime on the hips?" This is exactly where compounding will help improve your health. If you avoid the short-term pleasures that having an unhealthy treat will bring (similar to how you avoid withdrawing your interest from your investment to splurge on an impulsive purchase), you will gain long-term benefits.

When you make physical activity a consistent part of your lifestyle, you're investing in your long-term health and well-being. You're building a foundation of physical strength and resilience that will serve you well throughout your life. By following a workout programme consistently and making it a daily habit, you're creating a positive association with exercise that makes it easier to maintain in the long run. Just like with relationships, the key is to stay consistent and committed, and you'll be rewarded with a healthier, happier life.

Creating a comprehensive health blueprint that goes beyond just physical health is essential to achieving true wellness and abundance in life. By looking at all aspects of your health, from mental and emotional well-being to spiritual and social health, you'll be able to create a strong foundation for a fulfilling and prosperous life.

Compounding Finances

With traditional investing, you invest £100 at an annual interest rate of 10%. After the first year of investment, you will have made a £10 profit and will have £110 in the investment. You decide to re-invest for another year at an annual interest rate of 10%. If you stick to only your original capital investment, you will make another £10 in year two. Your total profit over two years will be £20. This continues each year, and after 20 years, you would have earned 20 x £10 = £200.

However, if you take your initial profit of £10 over the first year and compound it by investing it with your original amount, you will invest £110 during the second year. If you still make a 10% profit on this, your profit will be £21 after the second year. This shows an increase in profit of £1 on the exact same initial investment.

While this additional £1 doesn't appear to be a lot, imagine this over the same 20-year period. Your overall investment would increase to £/$672, whereas without the compound effect, it would only be £300, a more than 100% increase in your investment.

Even relatively modest investment sums, once compounded, would generate a significant increase in your investment compared to taking or spending the annual interest. Now, imagine your initial investment was £1,000 or £10,000:

- £1,000 would increase to £6,727
- £10,000 would increase to £67,727

If you invested either of the £1,000 or £10,000 amounts above for just 10 years and implemented the compound effect, you would have accumulated a significant investment over a 20-year period. The £1,000 invested each year for 10 years and then left to compound over 20 years would have increased to £48,059, and similarly, the £10,000 invested each year for 10 years and then left to compound over 20 years would have increased to £480,594.

Compounding is, therefore, a strategy that can help you reap huge rewards from seemingly insignificant actions. Simply put, every time you re-invest your interest in an original investment, your interest will increase.

Understanding Compound Interest and Inflation

It is important to consider the impact of inflation rates on your savings. Let's use a simple example to illustrate this.

Imagine you have £100 in a savings account that earns a 5% interest rate. After one year, your savings would grow to £105. However, if the inflation rate is 10%, the value of your increased savings of £105 will actually be worth less than the original purchasing power of your original investment of £100.

To be able to maintain the same purchasing power as the previous year, you would need to earn an interest rate of 10% per annum, and your investment would be worth £110 just to be able to have the same purchasing power as you did the year before.

Due to the 10% inflation rate, your new savings amount of £105 would only have the purchasing power of £94.50.

This example highlights the importance of considering inflation when making investment decisions. It is essential to aim for returns that outpace inflation to protect the value of your savings and maintain your purchasing power over time.

> *Remember:* Inflation can and will erode the value of your money, so it is important to consider it when assessing your savings and investments.

If you rely only on the interest earned from your savings, it can negatively impact your finances. The income you receive from accumulated interest might not be enough to cover the same expenses as before. Inflation directly affects your purchasing power, meaning that the money you have will not be able to buy the same amount of goods and services in the future. This applies to all type of savings you have, like saving for your child's education. If you invest your money at a rate lower than the inflation rate, the value of your money will decrease over time.

However, if you choose to compound your investments by reinvesting your interest, you can offset the effects of inflation on your purchasing power. When you reinvest your interest, your investment will grow at a faster pace compared to not reinvesting. This can help your money keep up with or even outpace inflation, allowing you to maintain or increase your purchasing power over time.

The Snowball Effect

Compounding can help to fight inflation and increase your investment portfolio; it is often referred to as the snowball effect. You will not only earn interest on your original investment but also on your accrued earnings from previous compounding periods. The more you add to your investment, the faster the snowball and your finances will grow.

While there are many financial institutions that offer compounding options on investments, it is essential to be aware of the necessary steps to take to make sure you get the maximum benefits from your compounding. These include:

- **Get an early start**: The sooner you start with your compounding investment, the better, as you will give yourself more time to invest and reinvest your accrued interest. When you do this, try not to make withdrawals from your investment, as this will limit your money's ability to grow over time.
- **Frequency of your compounding**: The frequency of compounding can have a significant impact on your investment growth. If you choose to compound your interest annually, you will have to wait a whole year to start experiencing the benefits of compounding. During this time, you'll only earn interest on your original investment. However, if you opt for a shorter compounding interval, like monthly, weekly, or even daily, you will start reaping the rewards of compounding much sooner. With a shorter interval, the investment on which you earn interest will grow at a faster rate.

- **Most investment platforms offer a compounding calculator**: This tool allows you to see the results of different compounding frequencies. By using the calculator, you can determine which compounding frequency will give you the most favourable outcomes for your investment. Choosing a higher frequency will help you accelerate your investment growth and achieve your financial goals more quickly.
- **Fixed return schemes**: Fixed return schemes are investment options where you can earn a predetermined rate of return on your investment over a specific period of time. These schemes are designed to provide stability and certainty in terms of the returns you can expect. Unlike some other investment options, fixed-return schemes offer a fixed interest rate or dividend payout, which means you know exactly how much you will earn from your investment. This can be particularly appealing to individuals who prefer a more predictable and low-risk investment strategy.

- **Using a professional, independent, and all-around market advisor or broker with a proven track record can play a crucial role in managing your investments effectively.** These experts have the knowledge and experience to guide you through the complexities of the investment landscape and help you make informed decisions. They can assess your financial goals, risk tolerance, and investment timeframe to develop a personalised investment strategy that aligns with your needs. A professional advisor or broker can provide valuable insights, conduct thorough research, and identify potential investment opportunities that you may not be aware of. They can also help you navigate market fluctuations and make adjustments to your portfolio when necessary.

CHAPTER 14:
Impact of True Wealth

You Have Control of Your Life

How you take control of your life is your choice, and where to start is your choice. You may be fabulous in some areas and not so in others, and *Wealth Beyond Money* is, in its purest form, balance across all areas of your life, creating the mind and habits required for you to achieve your desired outcomes.:

- **Embrace focused and positive thinking**: As you contemplate the transformative changes you wish for in your life, remember to harness the power of concentrated and optimistic thinking. Instead of extending your focus to the entire spectrum of steps required to complete your task, channel your energy into the immediate next step with the bigger vision in mind. This tailored approach turns a broad task into smaller, manageable steps, fostering a sense of accomplishment and positivity with each shift forward.

Remember: Celebrate success along the way.

- **Harness optimism**: As you navigate your journey, permeate your thoughts with positivity and optimism. At all times, consciously choose to adopt an optimistic perspective and practice empowering self-talk. Such an energetic mind puts you in the ideal emotional and mental state to surge ahead, regardless of the complexity of the journey.

Remember: Your potential is boundless, and you have the power to shape your own success.

- **Clarify your core values and beliefs**: Knowing who you are and understanding your deepest drivers play an integral role in shaping your identity. This knowledge simplifies decision-making and clarifies why you do what you do, guiding you to take the right steps towards achieving your goals. Remember, your core values define your authentic self. Establishing what that authentic you is will support you in creating the new authentic you if that is what you need to do. Living life with integrity is vital to *Wealth Beyond Money*, balance, and actions are driven by your values and beliefs.

> *Remember*: Do not be authentic to a damaging identity!

- **Create a vision**: As you embark on your journey of change, having a clearly defined vision provides you with direction and control. This vision serves as your golden thread, tying together your actions and experiences, and guiding you towards your ultimate goals. Visualise your future success—imagine what it looks like, sounds like, and feels like, and keep this image at the forefront of your mind. This powerful vision will be your true north compass, leading you forward and reinforcing your resilience in every step you take towards your future self.

> ***Remember***: Create your own vision otherwise you may achieve someone else's.

- **Celebrate change**: Embracing the exciting range of possibilities with your chosen life changes enhances your adaptability to face challenges gracefully and easily. It also opens up opportunities to identify the positive aspects of all transitions, bolstering your emotional resilience. Remember, to live well, you require a balance of certainty and uncertainty. By welcoming these self- and life-mastery shifts into your life, you create enriching experiences that foster growth and personal transformation.

> ***Remember:*** To be in balance there will be both positive and negative situations in life

- **Embrace clarity and evidence-based information**: As you navigate through your chosen changes, grounding yourself in the facts about these choices provides you with valuable insights and confidence. This includes understanding the rationale behind your decision to make this change, recognising its benefits, and knowing the specifics of this transformation. With clarity and evidence-based knowledge, you can confidently complete the change, supported by the fact that each step is purposeful and aligned with your objectives.

> *Remember*: The facts that led to the initial decision you made to adopt these changes.

- **Love progress over perfection**: If you find yourself striving for perfection, understand that the beauty of life often lies in its unpredictability and the lessons you learn through your unique journey. By willingly accepting that imperfections are an integral part of life's tapestry, you allow yourself to focus on your progress. This perspective enhances your adaptability to the dynamic nature of life's changes and empowers you to navigate your journey with greater ease and confidence.

> *Remember*: The concept of perfection is subjective and unique to the perspective and experiences of the beholder.

- **Maintain a healthy lifestyle**: Practice self-care throughout your journey; in fact, self-care may be your primary goal for achieving success and reaching your goals. Exercise, eating healthy, getting proper sleep, and eliminating bad habits will help you improve your overall wellness: physical, emotional, and mental.

Remember: Health is easier to maintain than recoup.

- **Craft a strategic action plan**: Having decided to introduce changes into your life, ensure that you are equipped with a clear, well-defined roadmap of the steps you need to take as well as their sequence. This approach equips you with a sense of direction and also provides you with control over your journey. Embrace a strategy that involves setting manageable, achievable steps. Smaller steps have the advantage of being less daunting, promoting steady progress while maintaining your confidence and momentum.

Remember: Access Setting Goals for Change by Julie Hogbin on Audible and Amazon to support you with this element it is a skill set and a mindset to create great Goals.

- **Draw strength from positive past experiences**: Whenever you embark on making new changes, bolster your confidence by recalling instances when you've successfully navigated similar transformations. Such reflections serve as powerful reminders of your capabilities and resilience. They reaffirm that just as your previous changes led to growth and benefits, your current journey of change also promises positive outcomes.

> *Remember:* Trust in your past achievements to fuel your future success.

- **Embrace mindful responding**: Instead of instantaneously reacting to a situation, allow yourself the grace of a moment to understand and manage your emotions before taking action. This approach cultivates mindfulness, giving you the space to compose yourself and decide how you wish to respond in a balanced and thoughtful manner. This practice of mindful responding places you in the driver's seat of your behaviour, paving the way for considered and constructive actions.

> *Remember:* Responding wins over reaction every time.

- **Leverage professional guidance**: Consider seeking assistance if navigating changes seems complex. Professionals like mentors and coaches can provide invaluable guidance, supporting and challenging you to manage your emotions and make sound progress on your transformation journey. Trusted friends or family members can offer you the necessary support and encouragement. Valuable external insights will unlock your potential unseen areas that may hold you back and will expand your ability to learn and grow.

Remember: Seeking help is a sign of strength and wisdom, not weakness.

- **Balance with well-timed breaks**: As you journey through your chosen changes, maintaining balance is essential by focusing on one task at a time and integrating refreshing breaks into your routine. This approach allows for a steady pace, energising you and maintaining your overall well-being. Well-timed breaks are vital energy boosters, helping you stay motivated and engaged while avoiding exhaustion.

Remember: Enjoy this journey of change with mindful pacing, knowing that balance is key to sustained progress.

You Set and Achieve Goals

The great danger for most of us lies not in setting our aim too high and falling short; but in setting our aim too low and achieving our mark.

–Michelangelo

Empowered and ready, you are now more than prepared to overcome obstacles, embrace change, take the reins of your life, and become your own sovereign. There are specific strategies to set and realise your goals effectively. Regardless of the nature of your aspirations linked to *Wealth Beyond Money*—personal, professional, or a blend of both—the approach to achieving them remains universal, underscoring the importance of consistency and determination in your journey towards success:

You are goal driven all of the time make them the ones you desire and design.

–Julie Hogbin

- **Define your outcomes**: If you haven't already defined your mission and vision, do it now, prior to setting any goals. Understand and articulate the outcomes you desire and aim for goals that foster balance in your life towards *Wealth Beyond Money*. This clear and aligned perspective guides you in setting relevant and meaningful goals and provides a continuous source of motivation to propel you forward. Remember, the foundation of every goal is a vision—let this vision be your shining light towards success.
- **Visualise achieving your goals**: The power of mental visualisation taps directly into your unconscious and significantly increases your achievement. Create a full vision and think about how you will feel when you have reached your goals. What emotions will you experience? What impact will reaching your goals have on your life? This is the vision of the new you in your new future in full sovereign power. Do not hold back, write it down, as well as create the image.

See it, Say it, Write it, Believe it, Achieve it.

–**Julie Hogbin**

- **Prioritise your goals**: Prioritise your goals according to their importance; focus on the vital few versus the trivial many; and identify which goals provide you with the best quality result. Prioritisation aids in navigating your goals more effectively, streamlining your journey towards success. This methodical approach contributes to efficient goal management and infuses a sense of balance and harmony in your pursuit of potentially diverse life objectives. It will also strengthen your drive and determination.

- **Set goals**: Follow the STRUCTURE method for the 21st century and beyond to set your goals and communicate them to yourself and to others who will support and challenge you. Create specific plans for how you will go about reaching your goals. Look at what steps you need to take to reach your goals and chunk the goals down into manageable steps. Create your own project plan; the more detailed it is, the better it will be.

Remember: Goals can be adjusted to suit, and they need to be a work in progress.

- **Create a timeline**: Set clear deadlines on when you want to complete each of the tasks on your journey to reaching your goals. Be realistic when you create your timeline and allow some buffer time in your schedule. It is perfectly normal for deadlines to slip; external influences happen that are out of your control. Accept it as normal, and even with delays, you will achieve your overall goals.

- **Identify obstacles**: It serves to identify what may get in your way, and a great tool for this is a SWOT analysis. SWOT stands for strengths, weaknesses, opportunities, and threats. The SW are internal factors directly relating to you, and the OT are related to the external environment. You can prepare for any obstacles you may face and plan what you can do to overcome them. When you are well prepared for the challenges you may face, you will know exactly what to do should they arise.

- **Follow your plan**: You have now created a detailed plan on the different steps you will take to reach your goal, as well as deadlines for when you want to achieve them. Now, put them into action and be strict with yourself about following your plan. You may benefit from discussing your plan with a trusted friend, family member, or even colleague who will be able to hold you accountable for the different steps you have set out for yourself.

- **Accept challenges as learning opportunities**: In your journey towards your goals, the emergence of challenges is a natural part of the process. Instead of viewing these moments as obstacles, shift your perspective to see them as unique opportunities for learning and growth. This mindset allows you to devise solutions and navigate these situations with ease. Rather than perceiving challenges as mistakes or failures, see them as invaluable learning experiences rich with insights that empower you to continually evolve and succeed.

- **Acknowledge every victory**: Remember that all progress is good progress, regardless of how small or large it is. Celebrate these victories and use them as motivation to continue on your journey to achieving your goals. Add the success to your win list and add gratitude for yourself and anyone who has supported you along the journey to your appreciation list.

- **Measure your success**: "If you can't measure it, you can't manage it," said Peter Drucker, and it is true. Ensure you have measurements as part of your STRUCTURE. When you can measure your goals, you will be able to see the successes you achieve on your journey. Acknowledge and record your progress and celebrate; this provides you with a direct line of sight to see the impact your changes have had on your life.

- **Evaluate and revise your plans regularly**: Even the best-thought-out plans may not be the ideal way to go about reaching your goals. On occasion, there may be things that happen outside of your control or influence that make it harder for you to follow your plans and reach your goals. When this happens, revisit your plans and SWOT analysis and establish what you can do differently to keep moving forward.

- **Develop perseverance**: Keep advancing steadfastly on your path to achieving your goals. Indeed, attaining some of them, particularly the long-term ones, may require substantial perseverance. Remember, each step forward, no matter how small, is a victory worth celebrating. These incremental triumphs fuel your motivation and pave the way to realising your ambitions. It is essential to have faith in yourself and to persist through the complexities of the journey, knowing that each challenge is simply a stepping stone to your ultimate success.

Establishing and pursuing goals is an essential catalyst for life-changing transformations and plays a vital role in shaping your life blueprint. When you define clear, purpose-driven goals, you essentially map out your desired path, with each goal serving as a landmark in your journey towards self-mastery.

As you progress and meet these goals, you are actively designing and scripting change, inching closer to the ideal blueprint of your life step-by-step.

Remember: Setting goals isn't merely a way of initiating and monitoring change; they drive your evolution across personal and professional spheres.

As you embark on this journey, remember that creating *Wealth Beyond Money* is the key to unlocking the life you truly desire and deserve. Take a moment to reflect on the reasons that sparked your desire for change and the adjustments you yearn to make to the blueprints of your life. By doing so, you open the door to a life that encompasses:

- **Living a life of fulfilment**: Imagine a life where every day is filled with a deep sense of purpose, joy, and contentment. True wealth goes beyond material possessions; it lies in pursuing activities, relationships, and endeavours that bring you genuine fulfilment and meaning. Embracing your passions, nurturing your talents, and pursuing the things that make you feel alive.

- **Living a life of wellness**: Your well-being is the foundation of a truly wealthy life. It encompasses physical, mental, and emotional health. Prioritise self-care, nourish your body with wholesome foods, engage in regular exercise, and practice mindfulness. By nurturing your overall well-being, you empower yourself to lead a life of vitality, resilience, and balance.

- **Living a life of contribution**: One of the most rewarding aspects of true wealth is the ability to make a positive impact on the world around you. Seek opportunities to give back, whether through acts of kindness, supporting charitable causes, or sharing your unique skills and talents. By contributing to the well-being of others, you experience a profound sense of fulfilment and create a legacy of compassion and generosity.

- **Living a life of choice**: True wealth allows you to live life on your own terms. It grants you the freedom to make choices aligned with your values, passions, and aspirations. Embrace the power of self-determination and cultivate the courage to pursue the path that resonates with your true self. Each decision you make brings you closer to a life filled with empowered purpose and integrity-led authenticity.

- **Living a life of abundance**: Abundance encompasses a mindset of gratitude and appreciation for the joy that already exists in your life. Shift your focus from scarcity to abundance, recognising the wealth of opportunities, love, relationships, and experiences that surround you. Embrace a mindset of abundance, and you will attract more positivity, joy, and prosperity into your life.

By making these changes and embracing the true essence of wealth, you not only transform your own life but also uplift the lives of those around you. Your journey towards *Wealth Beyond Money* will enrich your relationships, ignite a sense of purpose in others, and inspire a ripple effect of positive change. The wealth you create transcends and brings multidimensional wellness and prosperity to all.

With determination and a clear vision in mind, embark on this path of true wealth. Embrace the extraordinary possibilities that lie ahead and let the impact of your journey extend far beyond material riches. You can manifest a life of genuine wealth, and as you do, you will discover a world of fulfilment, wellness, contribution, choice, and abundant blessings that exceed all expectations.

Wealth Beyond Money Wellness Is Multi-Dimensional

Wellness extends far beyond the realm of physical health; it encompasses a holistic approach to improving every facet of your being. By nurturing your overall well-being, you pave the way for a life that is filled with vitality, happiness, and success. The different dimensions of wellness that contribute to your overall fulfilment are:

- **Emotional wellness**: Take the time to connect with your emotions and cultivate self-awareness. Embrace your feelings in all their glory and show compassion towards others. By fostering emotional intelligence, you create a solid foundation for deep and meaningful relationships.

- **Environmental wellness**: Create an environment that supports your personal growth and aligns with your aspirations. Surround yourself with positivity, whether it's through your physical surroundings or the people you choose to have in your life. Design a space that nurtures your well-being and encourages you to thrive.

- **Mental wellness**: Your mind is a powerful tool that holds the key to personal growth and expansion. Engage in continuous learning, challenge yourself to acquire new skills, and stimulate your intellect. By taking care of your mental health, you unlock your true potential and open doors to endless possibilities.

- **Physical wellness**: Your physical health is the cornerstone of your overall well-being. Nurture your body by adopting healthy habits such as regular exercise, nutritious eating, and sufficient rest. By prioritising your physical wellness, you energise yourself, boost your immune system, and enhance your longevity.

- **Social wellness**: Cultivate meaningful relationships and build a strong support system. Surround yourself with people who uplift and inspire you. Contribute to your community and make a positive impact on the lives of others. By nurturing your social connections, you enrich your own life and create a sense of belonging and purpose.

- **Financial Wellness**: Learn about money and what you can do with it. Uncover the belief systems you hold around it. Create your own financial freedom in a manner that serves you, knowing that you are secure and profitable in your own right. Know your numbers and live within your means, utilising good debt.

- **Spiritual wellness**: Seek a sense of purpose and meaning in your life. Connect with your inner self and explore your beliefs and values. Engage in practices that align with your spiritual journey, whether it's through meditation, mindfulness, or connecting with nature. By nurturing your spiritual wellness, you find a deeper sense of fulfilment and unleash your true potential.

The Impact of Wealth Beyond Money

> *Believe you can, and you're halfway there.*
> *–Theodore Roosevelt*

Now, let us revisit the impact of *Wealth Beyond Money*. As we have shared, true wealth encompasses the harmonious integration of physical, emotional, and mental well-being, healthy relationships, and financial health. Without meaningful connections and vibrant health, monetary wealth loses its purpose.

Your journey towards *Wealth Beyond Money* is an opportunity to manifest the life you desire, bridging the gap between where you are now and where you want to be. Manifestation means you do something differently; it is the connection between setting goals and achieving them.

Creating awareness is the first step in making any change in your life, including creating new blueprints within these three comprehensive aspects of your life. It is important to understand why you need to make certain changes and how they will impact your life for the better. Once you have identified the areas of your life that need improvement, take some time to consider the benefits that these improvements will bring. This is key because it will motivate you to adopt the changes necessary to achieve the results and outcomes you desire. With a clear understanding of the benefits of making changes, you can take action and begin transforming your life.

The definition of insanity is doing the same thing over and over and expecting different results.

–Albert Einstein

When implementing changes in your life, it is important to be patient with yourself. There may be times when you consciously remind yourself of the changes you have committed to making. It is important to stick with it.

> ***Remember:*** It takes, on average, 66 days for a new habit or behaviour to form and become automatic.

The more you consistently practise your new habit, the easier it will become. Stay on track, remind yourself why you are doing the *thing*, and before you know it, your new habit will be second nature.

As you journey towards wealth beyond money, it's important not to let discomfort become a crutch holding you back. Instead, actively seek out individuals who have achieved the success you desire or think differently than you do. Be open to learning from them and ask questions about how they have reached their level of success. Even though your circumstances may be different, you'll likely discover there's much you can learn from them.

A brief reminder!

Healthy Lifestyle

Your overall health is a precious asset that allows you to fully experience and enjoy your life. By embracing a healthy lifestyle, you improve your mood, increase your energy levels, and boost your overall well-being. A healthy body, inside and out, and mind provide the foundation for a vibrant and fulfilling existence.

Healthy Relationships

Meaningful relationships form the fabric of a rich and purposeful life. Cultivating healthy connections with yourself, your loved ones, and your professional network brings emotional support, reduces stress, and enhances your physical health. These relationships provide opportunities for personal growth and contribute to a deep sense of purpose and happiness.

Strong Finances

While money alone cannot guarantee happiness, it does provide you with choices and opportunities. Financial stability empowers you to pursue education, live life to the fullest, and make a positive impact on your community and the wider world. It grants you freedom, security, and the ability to differentiate between survival and thriving.

Now, Remember Chapter 4

Exercise: Create That Plan

In Chapter 4, we asked you to reflect on every area below:

- Areas for Improvement
- Areas to start
- Areas to stop
- Areas to continue

We also requested that you not beat yourself up, celebrate your success, and recognise that there are probably areas you can improve.

Now, we ask you to truly embrace the opportunity to design a remarkable blueprint for your future, one that encompasses all aspects of your life: health, nutrition, relationships, career, business, and finance.

Identify the areas that need improvement and the areas that already bring you joy and success.

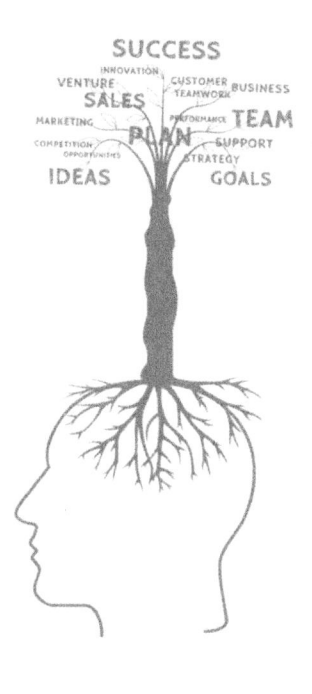

Set exciting goals and outline the actionable steps you will take to achieve them, utilising the STRUCTURE model.

Believe in the power of your beliefs and attitudes to shape your reality and commit to making positive changes in each area.

Prioritise your mental, emotional, and physical health by nurturing your body with nutritious choices and energising exercise.

Embrace the art of meaningful connections and effective communication, fostering relationships that bring fulfilment and purpose.

Seize the opportunities for growth and advancement in your business or career, fuelled by a burning passion and a relentless drive.

Take control of your finances, make wise choices that secure your future, and embrace abundance with an open heart, utilising Immanuel Ezekiel's book *The 6 Steps to Financial Freedom*.

Today is the day to create a comprehensive blueprint that reflects your dreams and inspires you to take bold action. Now, go forth and design a conscious life that surpasses your wildest expectations, for the power to shape your destiny lies within you.

CONCLUSION

Success is not final; failure is not fatal:
It is the courage to continue that counts.
—**Winston Churchill**

Now is the time to heed the call to action and Get Off Your Arse (GOYA). You possess the remarkable ability to create meaningful change and transform your life. Now, it is time to make that first decision, for even the longest journey begins with a single step.

This quest for *Wealth Beyond Money* requires creating balance and transforming goals into tangible achievements, and by doing so, you embark on a transformational path towards the life you desire. Take full ownership of your journey, knowing that regardless of your current circumstances, you have the ability to attain complete control of your life.

Embrace change and the discomfort it may bring, navigating through your emotions that arise during the process. Take ownership and acknowledge that your results are your choice, regardless of your current circumstances. Your past really does not determine your future when you are willing to change and expand your comfort zone. You have the extraordinary ability to write your story and to shape a life that radiates abundance in all its forms.

Visualise the life you desire with crystal clarity, painting a vivid picture of vibrant health, thriving relationships, and financial freedom. Picture the total freedom that empowers you to live life on your own terms. Allow this vision to guide you on your journey, fuelling your determination to make it a reality.

Recognise the significance of having comprehensive plans for every aspect of your life. Set structured goals, outline the steps to success that are necessary, and create a timeline, allowing room for flexibility. Life happens.

Remember that progress is not solely measured by grand leaps but by the consistency and compounding of your actions. Embrace the power of each action you take, for they are the building blocks of your success, and commit to continuous progress, knowing that each step builds your transformation and growth.

Avoid the trap of comparing yourself to others, which can steal joy and hinder your progress. It is vital to remember that you are on your own unique path, and it is essential to recognise that you are in control of your own destiny. Refuse to be defined by society's labels or limitations; break free from imposed expectations, yours, and anyone else's.

Reprogram your mind to align with success and set yourself up for a fulfilling future.

Remember, you possess all the keys to unlocking *Wealth Beyond Money*. Embrace the principles, examine the blueprints you currently possess, determine the changes needed, take inspired action, and persist with unwavering belief in yourself. It is absolutely within your reach to achieve the abundance you seek. Trust your journey, stay focused, and remember that greatness lies within your grasp.

Celebrate every milestone, no matter how small, and with each passing day, reaffirm your commitment to yourself. Believe in your abilities, your resilience, and your power to create the life you envision.

Continue your journey by revisiting the insights and tips shared in this book. Allow them to guide and inspire you. With determination and perseverance, you are capable of achieving the remarkable life you deserve. Believe in yourself and embrace the boundless possibilities that lie ahead.

In conclusion, embarking on the journey to true *Wealth Beyond Money* is a quest for balance, a harmonious integration of everything from health to relationships to finance. By creating this equilibrium, you pave the way for a joyous and remarkably successful life where you transform your goals into tangible achievements.

We want to ignite a spark within you by sharing our wisdom and inspiring you to take consistent action every day, committing and recommitting to your journey. Believe wholeheartedly in your abilities, resilience, and capacity to shape your own destiny.

Along your journey, draw inspiration from these powerful thoughts:

The only limits in life are the ones you set in your head.

and

The best way to predict your future is to create it.

You possess all the keys to unlocking *Wealth Beyond Money*. Embrace the principles, take inspired action, and persist with unwavering belief in yourself. It is absolutely within your reach to achieve the abundance you seek. Trust in your journey, design your process, stay focused, and remain steadfast in your pursuit of the extraordinary possibilities that lie ahead. *Wealth Beyond Money* lies in your grasp.

ABOUT THE AUTHORS

Immanuel Ezekiel

Millionaire, Property Investor, Author, Business Consultant, High-Performance Coach, and Master NLP Practitioner.

From humble beginnings to soaring heights of success, Immanuel has blazed a trail of financial triumph, resilience, and unwavering determination. As a millionaire property investor, author, business consultant, and high-performance coach, he was featured on Channel 5's "Rich House, Poor House" programme and recognised as the best Investment Pitch on Sky TV's "Property Elevator" for his exemplary investment acumen.

IMMANUEL EZEKIEL & JULIE HOGBIN

With a passion for health and fitness, Immanuel defies age, boasting the physique of a remarkable 20-year-old. In his 7th decade, he defies conventional expectations, boasting a physique that rivals individuals decades younger. This unwavering dedication to wellness underlines his belief in the inseparable connection between financial prosperity and the vitality of mind, body, and soul.

Despite facing adversity, living in poverty, and leaving school with minimal qualifications at the tender age of sixteen, Immanuel's indomitable spirit led him to embark on an extraordinary journey of self-education. Imbued with an insatiable thirst for knowledge, he devoured books, traversed the globe to attend enlightening seminars, and absorbed the wisdom found in thought-provoking teachings. This unyielding pursuit of self-improvement laid the foundation for his extraordinary success.

Drawing from his newfound knowledge, Immanuel established a thriving financial management company, overseeing a team of 100 professionals and generating annual sales exceeding £7 million. His relentless dedication to success led him to amass shares in a portfolio of over 200 properties valued at an impressive £50 million. His journey from rags to riches stands as a testament to the power of vision, perseverance, and a commitment to lifelong learning.

In his groundbreaking book, *The 6 Steps To Financial Freedom*, Immanuel has meticulously developed a proven formula, empowering individuals burdened with significant debt with the tools, mindset, and strategies to transform their lives at an unimaginable pace. Through his financial management company and his tried-and-true techniques, he has already assisted thousands of individuals in eliminating debt, building wealth, and attaining financial freedom in record time.

For links, articles, information, and programme information, visit www.ImmanuelEzekiel.com.

Rise Above Challenges, for They Are Stepping Stones to Success and Growth.

–Immanuel Ezekiel

Client Testimonials

"I was trapped in a seemingly endless cycle of debt, feeling overwhelmed and hopeless about my financial situation. That's when I discovered Immanuel Ezekiel, the financial wizard and money management consultant who completely transformed my life."

"Immanuel's direct, no-nonsense approach cut through all the BS and got straight to the heart of the matter. His deep understanding of finance and business allowed him to guide me through the most challenging financial situations with ease. He not only helped me navigate the stormy waters but also empowered me to make informed decisions that led to significant positive outcomes."

"Working with Immanuel was a game-changer. His expertise and insight have enabled me to not only overcome my financial struggles but also achieve remarkable success. His ability to work with businesses, business owners, high-net-worth clients, and sophisticated investors is truly remarkable. With his guidance, I have witnessed safe and high returns on my capital and investments like never before."

"Immanuel Ezekiel's impact on my life goes far beyond finances. His unwavering dedication and passion for helping others break free from the chains of debt and attain financial independence have inspired me to dream bigger, set higher goals, and push myself to new heights. He is not just a consultant; he is a mentor, a motivator, and a true catalyst for personal growth."

"Are you ready to break free from the chains of debt and achieve financial independence? If you want to engage Immanuel Ezekiel, the financial wizard, money management consultant, and business advisor who can transform your life. With his direct, no-nonsense approach and unwavering dedication to your success, Immanuel can guide you through any difficult financial situation and help you achieve safe and high returns on your capital or investments."

"Take the first step towards your journey to Wealth Beyond Money and financial freedom today and experience the magic that Immanuel Ezekiel brings to the table."

Remember: Your path to a brighter financial future starts with a single step. Your life will never be the same.

Julie Hogbin

Multi-published Author, Podcaster, Mentor, Human Behaviourist, Leadership Consultant, NLP Practitioner and Emotional Change Therapist.

Author Page	Podcast

Julie's life journey has been an adventure of growth and transformation. Throughout her extraordinary journey, she has worn various hats, from accounting to audit, becoming a multi-published author and a seasoned property investor, mining crypto along the way. For over three decades, she has honed her skills in the Human Behaviour Personal Development field as a Leadership Consultant and has had the privilege of touching the lives of over 20,000 individuals.

Throughout her remarkable journey, starting from leaving the education system the first day she legally could, Julie has ventured across the globe, immersing herself in diverse cultures and connecting with people from all walks of life. Her insatiable appetite for knowledge and her genuine interest in understanding different perspectives have allowed her to establish a broad and inclusive outlook on Leadership and holistic wealth creation. From the busy streets of cities to the serene landscapes of remote villages, Julie has embraced the wisdom of each culture she has encountered. She has learned valuable lessons from the individuals considered poor financially and wealthy in other areas and from the billionaires that, although they are financially rich, they are poor in many other areas. She has learned and increased her wisdom from both ends of the spectrum, which she shares willingly.

By traversing the world and learning from the richness of human experience, Julie has become a true global citizen, embodying the essence of unity and interconnectedness in her teachings on Conscious Leadership for Business and Life and the boundless potential of holistic abundance.

A true embodiment of integrity, Julie walks the talk, is straightforward in her approach, and is compassionate in her interactions. Her guiding principles are designed with intention, and she has a visionary spirit and way of thinking that have grown with age rather than dimmed. Julie is truly motivational and inspiring; her warmth and positive energy are infectious, and she leaves the companies and individuals she chooses to work with safe, secure, and in a much better place.

With her unwavering belief in karma, the universe, and the interconnectivity of all things, Julie understands the profound influence of our actions on the world, ourselves, our businesses, and those around us, and that everything in life is intertwined.

We are sovereign beings, holding the key to our ultimate power and ultimate destiny. When we grasp the *why* and the *how*, we possess the capacity to effect profound and positive transformation.

With a forward-focused mindset and unwavering confidence, she wholeheartedly embraces the notion that all have the ability to achieve greatness, whatever that greatness means for the individual.

Julie takes immense pride in her life and is the creator of The Conscious Leadership Code, a transformative journey from *Intention to Impact*; *The Leadership Voice—The Art of Transparency*, a powerful framework for cultivating integrity-led leadership; and the DREAM model of coaching, among others.

These frameworks are tools that unlock the extraordinary potential and power residing within each of you to lead a life of purpose, passion, and profit with integrity for yourself and others.

As the host of the Conscious Leadership Podcast, Julie's voice resonates with leaders worldwide, and she has often been described as the *voice on the shoulder* when clarity and confidence are required and when the thought of "What would Julie do and say?" springs to mind. Of course, she is vitally proud of her books on Amazon and Audible.

For links, articles, information, and programme information, visit https://juliehogbin.com/ or her Amazon Author page.

Website

Amazon Author Page

Everything is connected, nothing sits in isolation.

– Julie Hogbin

Client Testimonials

"Julie is a phenomenon. She is honest, wise, knowledgeable, and completely dedicated to helping individuals and companies develop and grow to be the best they can be. Multi-skilled with a depth of knowledge seldom found in one person. Cannot recommend her highly enough."

"I was incredibly fortunate to be able to take part in Julies Transparency and Communication program, where she coached us to look at all of our communication and how things that have happened in our lives have moulded us into both good and bad habits in all the ways of communication. It has really helped me in communicating with people and helped me to understand and see things from the other person's perspective. Personally, Julie is an amazing woman with a huge heart, a rod of professionalism and driven by a desire to help people be the best that they can be."

"Julie is a veritable expert in the field of leadership, personal development, training and learning. Her Conscious Leadership podcast is a real 'go-to' for me when I am looking for inspiration, motivation, and a different way of looking at the world."

"Julie is a fantastic coach and trainer. She developed, trained, and supported teams in their management practices, often turning around dysfunctional teams. Managers would walk out of training courses, saying it is the best course they have ever been on. They would praise Julie's training style highly. Julie is brilliant at listening and gives feedback transparently. She challenges managers' behaviours in training and in 1-1s without fear and supports them in realising what it is they have to do to improve or change."

Why We Created the Book

As the co-authors Immanuel Ezekiel and Julie Hogbin reflect on the journey that led us to collaborate on writing the book "Wealth Beyond Money," we are filled with gratitude for the unique circumstances that brought us together.

Our writing partnership was forged during the challenging days of the COVID-19 pandemic, which serves as an example that even though people were not allowed to gather together physically they could connect on line on the voice platforms that sprang up and serves as a testament to the power of technology and the human spirit, the need for connection and community brought people together who would never have met and that was worldwide.

The conversations on Clubhouse, most mornings, sparked an interest and a respect for each other and over about a year Julie listening to Immanuel in the gym at home whilst sharing his depth of knowledge and Immanuel liking the energy, professionalism and messages that Julie shared.

A synchronicity of missions evolved with shared values and a deep belief that we are all capable of being in balance and that something stops many from accessing that magic.

We are both distinguished in our respective fields; however, our paths had never crossed until we found ourselves on the Clubhouse app during those confused times. It was an era marked by isolation and uncertainty, yet it was within these digital spaces that we discovered a shared passion and a common mission.

From the very beginning, it was clear that our combined knowledge and skills complemented each other in a remarkable way. Our synergy was unmistakable, as if the universe itself had orchestrated our meeting. Immanuel made the 1st move and Julie didn't hesitate – writing is a passion and can be a single pursuit so to write with a complimentary soul with completely different life experiences was a joy – fate had intervened and to think with Clubhouse and without lockdown they would never have met – well maybe not!

However, what truly bound us together was our unwavering commitment to helping people. We recognised that the challenges posed by the pandemic were not merely isolated issues of health, relationships or finances. Instead, we saw the interconnectedness of these aspects in shaping a person's overall well-being. We were determined to create a lasting resource, a timeless guide that would transcend the immediate crises of the pandemic and remain relevant for generations to come.

The book "Wealth Beyond Money" was born out of this shared vision. We have poured our hearts and souls into distilling our expertise into its pages, crafting a roadmap for readers to navigate the intricate web of health, relationships, and money. We know that the principles and fundamentals that we shared have the power to transform lives, not just for today but for a century and beyond.

As we recall the incredible journey that brought us together, we are reminded of the profound impact that collaboration, even in the most unexpected of circumstances, can have on the world. Our story serves as a reminder that, when driven by passion and a genuine desire to help others, the bonds formed in times of adversity can lead to remarkable creations that stand the test of time.

REFERENCES

A quote by Dalai Lama XIV. (n.d.). GoodReads. https://www.goodreads.com/quotes/ 885801-the-dalai-lama-when-asked-what-surprised-him-most-about

A quote by Steve Jobs. (n.d.). GoodReads. https://www.goodreads.com/quotes/ 412696-i-have-looked-in-the-mirror-every-morning-and-asked

Alexander, A. (2012, September 14). *10 powerful benefits of change and why we should embrace it.* Tiny Buddha. https://tinybuddha.com/blog/10-powerful-benefits-of- change-why-embrace-it/

Antonatos, L. (2023, March 16). *Fear of change: Causes, getting help, and ways to cope.* Choosing Therapy. https://www.choosingtherapy.com/fear-of-change/

Axelrod, S. (2023, February 24). *Set goals and achieve them.* WikiHow. https://www.wikihow.com/Set-Goals-and-Achieve-Them

Benefits of physical activity. (2022, April 27). Centers for Disease Control and Prevention. https://www.cdc.gov/physicalactivity/basics/pa-health/index.htm

Chakavarti, A. (n.d.). *What is power of compounding?* Max Life Insurance. https://www.maxlifeinsurance.com/blog/investments/5-ways-you-can-improve-your-savings-through-the-power-of-compounding

Chatterjee, A. (2023, January 31). *Financial freedom: Simple 9 steps to achieve it.* ET Money Learn. https://www.etmoney.com/learn/mutual-funds/9-steps-to-achieve-financial-freedom/

Clear, J. (2018, July 13). *How long does it actually take to form a new habit?* James Clear. https://jamesclear.com/new-habit

Compounding (snowball effect). (n.d.). Model Thinkers. https://modelthinkers.com/ mental-model/compounding-snowball-effect

Credihealth. (2023, January 17). *Growth hormone deficiency- A game of life won by Lionel Messi.* Credihealth Blog. https://www.credihealth.com/blog/lionel-messi-growth-hormone-deficiency/

Eatough, E. (2022, August 31). *The 8 stages of life: What can we learn from each one?* Better Up. https://www.betterup.com/blog/stages-of-life

Egan, J. (2022, November 3). *7 tips for financial success.* Experian. https://www.experian.com/blogs/ask-experian/tips-for-financial-success/

Fear of change: 6 ways to overcome fear of change. (2022, May 31). Masterclass. https://www.masterclass.com/articles/fear-of-change

Franklin D. Roosevelt - The first term. (2020). In Encyclopædia Britannica. https://www.britannica.com/biography/Franklin-D-Roosevelt/The-first-term

Functions of money, economic lowdown podcasts. (n.d.). Federal Reserve Bank of St Louis. https://www.stlouisfed.org/education/economic-lowdown-podcast-series /episode-9-functions-of-money

Ginsberg, L. (2017, May 28). *Mark Zuckerberg, Richard Branson and Mark Cuban all agree that this one habit is key to success.* CNBC. https://www.cnbc.com/2017/05/28/mark-zuckerberg-and-richard-branson-exercise-is-key-to-success.html

Gordon, C. (2018, January 22). *5 steps to change your money blueprint.* LinkedIn. https://www.linkedin.com/pulse/5-steps-change-your-money-blueprint-cherrick-gordon-/

Harv Eker, T. (2018, February 9). *T. Harv Eker's top 10 tips for wealth and success.* LinkedIn. https://www.linkedin.com/pulse/harv-ekers-top-10-tips-wealth- success-t-harv-eker/

Harv Eker, T. (2019, July 29). *Money blueprints: How to get on the same page with your significant other.* Million Dollar Life Lessons. https://www.harveker.com/blog/money-blueprints-with-significant-other/

Hayes, A. (2022, July 11). *What is financial leverage, and why is it important?* Investopedia. https://www.investopedia.com/terms/l/leverage.asp#toc- advantages-of-leverage

How to change your money blueprint. (2016, April 25). Life Coach Directory. https://www.lifecoach-directory.org.uk/memberarticles/how-to-change-your-money-blueprint

Jim Rohn quotes. (n.d.). BrainyQuote. https://www.brainyquote.com/quotes/jim_rohn_121282

Jobs, S. (n.d.). *"You've got to find what you love."* Stanford|News. https://news.stanford.edu/2005/06/12/youve-got-find-love-jobs-says/

Kiyosaki, R. (2022, April 19). *Rich dad fundamentals: The cashflow quadrant.* Rich Dad. https://www.richdad.com/the-cashflow-quadrant

Kumar, A. (2020, June 4). *This is what happens when you know your blueprints in life.* Live Your Life on Purpose. https://medium.com/live-your-life-on-purpose/ this-is-what-happens-when-you-know-your-blueprints-in-life-ebcf614a02e9

Kunmar, A. (n.d.). *This is what happens when you know your blueprints in life.* Medium. https://medium.com/live-your-life-on-purpose/this-is-what-happens-when-you-know-your-blueprints-in-life-ebcf614a02e9

Levin, N. (2018, August 1). *How to determine your relationship blueprint?* Nancy Levin. https://nancylevin.com/how-to-determine-your-relationship-blueprint/

Li, P. (2020, January 2). *Classical conditioning and examples.* Parenting for Brain. https://www.parentingforbrain.com/classical-conditioning/

McLeod, S. (2018, December 20). *Nature vs. nurture in psychology.* Simply Psychology. https://www.simplypsychology.org/naturevsnurture.html

National Institutes of Health. (2021, August 26). *Social wellness toolkit.* National Institutes of Health (NIH). https://www.nih.gov/health-information/social-wellness-toolkit

National institutes of health. (2022, December 8). *Physical wellness toolkit.* National Institutes of Health (NIH). https://www.nih.gov/health-information/physical-wellness-toolkit

Personal Change Stages - John Fisher. (n.d.). BusinessBalls. https://www.businessballs.com/change-management/personal-change-stages-john-fisher/

Quotes (Dalai Lama XIV). (n.d.). Goodreads. https://www.goodreads.com/quotes/885801-the-dalai-lama-when-asked-what-surprised-him-most-about

Raton, B. (2009, April 24). *Your ego is your enemy.* Boca Raton, FL Therapists. https://www.bocaratoncounselingcenter.com/blog/115872-your-ego-is-your-enemy

Robbins, T. (2017, February 9). *6 strategic tips to reprogram your mind.* Tony Robbins. https://www.tonyrobbins.com/mind-meaning/how-to-reprogram-your-mind/

Robbins, T. (2021, May 12). *The power of leverage in business and personal life.* Tony Robbins. https://www.tonyrobbins.com/career-business/the-power-of-leverage /amp/

Roth, J. D. (2017, December 5). *Your money blueprint -- and how it shapes your world.* Get Rich Slowly. https://www.getrichslowly.org/money-blueprint/

7 great reasons why exercise matters. (2021, October 8). Mayo Clinic. https://www.mayoclinic.org/healthy-lifestyle/fitness/in-depth/exercise/art-20048389

Segeren, M. (2021, October 7). *Examples of social health.* Better You. https://www.betteryou.ai/examples-of-social-health/

Strategic Learning. (n.d.). CalPolyPomona. https://www.cpp.edu/eoda-hr/departments/strategic-learning/index.shtml

Thangavelu, P. (2023, February 7). *How inflation affects your savings.* Investopedia. https://www.investopedia.com/articles/investing/090715/how-inflation-affects-your-cash-savings.asp

University of Exeter. (n.d.). *The change curve.* https://www.exeter.ac.uk/media/universityofexeter/humanresources/documents/learningdevelopment/the_change_curve.pdf

What is wellness? (2019). Global Wellness Institute. https://globalwellnessinstitute.org /what-is-wellness/

Image References

Clker-Free-Vector-Images. (n.d.). *Gear Cog Wheel.* Pixabay. https://pixabay.com/vectors/gear-cog-wheel-tools-rack-wheel-307780/

Clker-Free-Vector-Images. (n.d.). *Idea Cloud Think.* Pixabay. https://pixabay.com/vectors/idea-cloud-think-concept-symbol-48100/

Clker-Free-Vector-Images. (n.d.). *People Group Silhouette.* Pixabay. https://pixabay.com/vectors/people-group-silhouette-team-309068/

Clker-Free-Vector-Images. (n.d.). *Puppy Face Nature.* Pixabay. https://pixabay.com/vectors/puppy-face-dog-pet-animal-mammal-294298/

GDJ, (n.d.). *Fingerprint Justice Scales.* Pixabay. https://pixabay.com/vectors/fingerprint-justice-scales-morality-7900106/

GDJ, (n.d.). *Heart Love Fingerprint.* Pixabay. https://pixabay.com/vectors/heart-love-fingerprint-swirls-2750394/

GDJ, (n.d.). *Woman Books Metamorphosis.* Pixabay. https://pixabay.com/vectors/woman-books-metamorphosis-change-7717172/

GDJ. (n.d.). *Cranium Head Human.* Pixabay. https://pixabay.com/vectors/cranium-head-human-male-man-2099128/

GDJ. (n.d.). *Neural Network Communication Intelligence.* Pixabay. https://pixabay.com/vectors/neural-network-communication-3322580/

GDJ. (n.d.). *One Inclusiveness Unity.* Pixabay. https://pixabay.com/vectors/one-inclusiveness-unity-united-3717696/

GDJ. (n.d.). *Sports Athletics Athletes.* Pixabay. https://pixabay.com/vectors/sports-athletics-athletes-exercise-2952560/

Geralt. (n.d.). *Clock Stopwatch Pay.* Pixabay. https://pixabay.com/vectors/clock-stopwatch-pay-digits-time-7259409/

Geralt. (n.d.). *Question Mark A Notice Duplicate.* Pixabay. https://pixabay.com/illustrations/question-mark-a-notice-duplicate-2153533/

Geralt. (n.d.). *Question Who How.* Pixabay. https://pixabay.com/illustrations/question-who-how-what-where-when-2415069/

Hassan, M. (n.d.). *Bird Cage Silhouette.* Pixabay. https://pixabay.com/vectors/bird-cage-silhouette-escape-3879179/

Hassan, M. (n.d.). *Yin Yang Harmony Balance.* Pixabay. https://pixabay.com/vectors/yin-yang-harmony-balance-silhouette-4401011/

Hain, J. (n.d.). *Mindset Stimulus Response.* Pixabay. https://pixabay.com/illustrations/mindset-stimulus-response-emotion-2113092/

Tyl, K. (n.d.). *Heart Love Relationship.* Pixabay. https://pixabay.com/vectors/heart-love-relationship-2466384/

Marquetand. (n.d.). *Circuits Brain Network.* Pixabay. https://pixabay.com/vectors/circuits-brain-network-chip-5076887/

Masks Masquerade Masque. (n.d.) Pixabay. https://pixabay.com/vectors/masks-masquerade-masque-faces-40963/

MCvec. (n.d.). *Sports Fitness Silhouette.* Pixabay. https://pixabay.com/vectors/sports-fitness-silhouette-workout-1975689/

OpenClipart-Vectors. (n.d.). *Adult Age Baby.* Pixabay. https://pixabay.com/vectors/adult-age-baby-child-death-human-2028245/

OpenClipart-Vectors. (n.d.). *Allergy Art Crying.* Pixabay. https://pixabay.com/vectors/allergy-art-crying-drawing-eye-1299884/

OpenClipart-Vectors. (n.d.). *Bank Buy Card royalty-free.* Pixabay. https://pixabay.com/vectors/bank-buy-card-credit-credit-card-1300155/

OpenClipart-Vectors. (n.d.). *Linked Connected Network.* Pixabay. https://pixabay.com/vectors/linked-connected-network-team-men-152575/

OpenClipart-Vectors. (n.d.). *Luck Rainbow Gold.* Pixabay. https://pixabay.com/vectors/luck-rainbow-gold-pot-152048/

OpenClipart-Vectors. (n.d.). *Telescope View Binocular.* Pixabay. https://pixabay.com/vectors/telescope-view-binocular-look-2027679/

OpenClipart-Vectors. (n.d.). *Writing Literature Feather.* Pixabay. https://pixabay.com/vectors/writing-literature-feather-quill-146913/

13smok. (n.d.). *Bag Cord Gold.* Pixabay. https://pixabay.com/vectors/bag-cord-gold-coins-treasure-3193388/

Smoke and Mirrors. (n.d.). Px Fuel. https://www.pxfuel.com/en/free-photo-xhoir

StarGladeVintage. (n.d.). *Chain Slavery Oppression*. Pixabay. https://pixabay.com/vectors/chain-slavery-oppression-jail-5596267/

Plus, originals by Julie Hogbin & Immanuel Ezekiel